William Keegan
Britain Without Oil

Penguin Books

Penguin Books Ltd, Harmondsworth, Middlesex, England
Viking Penguin Inc., 40 West 23rd Street, New York, New York 10010, U.S.A.
Penguin Books Australia Ltd, Ringwood, Victoria, Australia
Penguin Books Canada Ltd, 2801 John Street, Markham, Ontario, Canada L3R 1B4
Penguin Books (N.Z.) Ltd, 182–190 Wairau Road, Auckland 10, New Zealand

First published 1985

Made and printed in Great Britain by
Richard Clay (The Chaucer Press) Ltd, Bungay, Suffolk
Filmset in 10/13 pt Monophoto Photina by
Northumberland Press Ltd, Gateshead, Tyne and Wear

To my daughters
Clemency and Benedicta

Contents

Acknowledgements

Most of the people who helped my researches for this book and its predecessor, *Mrs Thatcher's Economic Experiment*, are government officials and politicians whose careers would not be assisted by a specific public acknowledgement. They know who they are, and I am deeply indebted to them all.

I should also like to thank Sir Ian Gilmour, Anthony Howard, Adrian Hamilton and Dr Ray Richardson for their generous encouragement and invaluable criticism.

Introduction

This book is concerned primarily with the relevance of North Sea oil to the British economy as a whole. There are already a number of works that describe the impact on the oil industry and on the Scottish economy. Detailed production figures and forecasts for individual fields are readily available from several sources, including the Department of Energy, stockbrokers Wood, Mackenzie and the Royal Bank of Scotland.

The direct economic impact of the North Sea – outside the effect on the balance of payments, government revenues and economic policy generally – has been remarkably small. The direct employment effects are calculated by the Manpower Services Commission at some 60,000 plus related jobs (full and part-time) amounting to whole-time equivalents of 20,000 or so.

The work and employment generated by the North Sea have been confined largely to the area of Aberdeen and the Shetlands. The impact on the economy of Scotland appears to have been no more than to offset part of the recessionary effect that Scotland, in common with the rest of the UK, has suffered in recent years.

Probably more important to Scotland, in terms of output and jobs, has been the attraction of new industries during recent years, partly as a result of the Government's earlier regional policies.

The North Sea brought work to Scotland during the exploratory phase through the construction of platforms, modules and landfall terminals for oil and gas and the servicing of North Sea oil platforms. The proportion of orders and construction work going to British firms from the North Sea appears to have been significantly below that implied by the Government's claim that 70 per cent has gone to UK companies.

This statistic includes UK subsidiaries of foreign firms: the bulk of the orders created by North Sea activity appears to have gone to US firms. Even French companies have done better out of the North Sea than domestic industry in exploiting the market for rigs, terminal installations and service contracts. And the North Sea has not led to the building up of a sizeable UK export industry based on a hoped-for competitive advantage in oil.[1]

PART ONE

PART ONE

1 Britain Before Oil

Britain is not without oil and will not be for a very long time. But the country's response to this great geological windfall – possession of its own oil – has been closely associated with its handling of the economy generally; and I shall argue that the man in the street is close to the truth in believing – as, in my experience, he certainly does – that the Government's handling of the North Sea has been shortsighted and negligent.

I hope to demonstrate, however, that the principal charge against the Government is not just the mishandling of policy towards oil. I suspect, for instance, that there are many more people who think the Government has been more mistaken in its attitude towards oil than in its attitude towards the general economy. This is in part, I believe, because of forgivable ignorance on the part of the public about what it regards as a rather arcane subject, but it is also because the Thatcher Government has been especially skilful both in its original identification of public concerns and in its subsequent defensive propaganda when things did not turn out quite as promised.

This skill lay originally, during the Opposition years of 1974–9 and the early years of office, in identifying public concern about the assumed power of the trade unions, and capitalizing on the general feeling that Britain was not economically productive enough. The latter was encapsulated in such statements as 'People aren't doing an honest day's work for an honest day's pay.' There is enough guilt within most of us for such allegations to strike home; and there is enough malice in all of us to agree that, even if we think we are doing a good job, the other fellow is not. In office, however, as I have described elsewhere,[1] the Conservatives proceeded, while purporting to solve the country's fundamental economic problems, to aggravate them severely. They risked throwing out the economic baby with the bath water.

After that the skill lay in making the best of things. The recovery was said to be 'around the corner' when it patently was not; unemployment was said to be about to fall when it was about to rise sharply; even when it was clear that the rise in unemployment had exceeded even the wildest dreams of the most savage 'union bashers', government propagandists told us, 'The shake-out was needed anyhow – we all knew that.'

Most important of all, however, this Government – which, in the words of its leaders, wished 'to shift the ground' of British politics – succeeded, for a long time, in transforming the way in which economic policy was discussed and conducted: the core of Keynesian economics was the belief that Governments could and should intervene to stabilize the economy and to maintain a reasonably high level of demand and activity – to stimulate when output and employment were flagging, to calm it down if the economy was showing symptoms of fever or overheating.

Mrs Thatcher and her ministerial colleagues long managed to tread on the very idea that Governments were, or ought to be, responsible for taking action to stimulate the economy. Their credibility eventually began to be questioned when it became clear, in spring 1985, that the much vaunted 'recovery' was not making a significant dent in the unemployment figures, and the man in the street was beginning to say, 'Something is going to go wrong when the oil runs out.'

This latter view is based on the simple – and, up to a point, reasonable – view that when the revenue stops coming in, and when the oil ceases to flow, then the Government is going to have less revenue (hence will impose higher taxes) and we are all going to have to produce more to pay for the oil we are not now having to import.

What is actually going to happen, on all the known evidence and most reasonable assumptions, is not a dramatic fall in the Government's oil revenues but a discontinuation of the rise. These revenues rose sixfold over the six-year period 1979/80 to 1984/85 to some £12 billion, or nearly one-tenth of the Chancellor's Budget. The main point is that they are projected to stop rising in the financial year 1985/86, when they are forecast to reach £13.5 billion, after which they will at best stabilize for a time before gently declining. Indeed, the 1985 Budget Report assumes they will fall by £2 billion a year, in both 1986/87 and 1987/88, to £9.5 billion.

It was only because of the huge surge in oil revenues that the Government was able, in its own terms, to balance the books. If things were deteriorating so fast elsewhere in the accounts, then this gush of oil revenues was vital. The revised fear of the man in the street must be that things will continue to deteriorate, without that offsetting improvement. So where are we now?

In both cases this approach takes a misleadingly static view of the economy – a view that the entire weight of recent government policy has, until recently, encouraged. For what was going on while the oil revenues were rising was an erosion of the tax base elsewhere in the economy. During the years 1979–81 gross domestic product (GDP: the nation's output of goods and services fell by 4 per cent in volume and manufacturing output by 20 per cent. Although £10 billion to £12 billion a year of oil revenues seems to be a windfall that has been 'wasted' on extra unemployment benefit and the like, if the output of the economy had grown at anything like its previous rate, there would not only have been less unemployment on which to 'squander' the oil money but there would also have been several times as much non-oil money again in extra tax revenues from a larger economic and industrial base.

In the course of 1984–5 the Government began to play down the significance of North Sea oil revenues, trying to emphasize that they were only a small proportion of total government revenues anyway. But it was going to be more difficult to calm worries about the implications for the balance of payments of the rundown of the North Sea. Net trade in oil had still been in deficit to the extent of £2 billion in 1978 and subsequently rose from a small surplus of £0.25 billion in 1980 to one of £7 billion in 1983 and £10 billion (official forecast) for 1985.

Meanwhile the trend of the manufacturing trade balance had deteriorated from a traditional surplus in the 1970s – albeit a declining one – to the first peacetime manufacturing deficit in history in 1983 (minus £2.5 billion). The obvious cause for concern was that the trade surplus in oil was now no longer expected to go on rising – 1985 was assumed in the Budget Report to be the peak. The only question is at what rate it will decline. Meanwhile, if the manufacturing side continues to deteriorate – and there is certainly no sign that services or other 'invisible' earnings will immediately fill the gap – then severe balance of payments trouble is in store. The balance of payments will always in some sense 'balance'. What matters is the exchange rate and level of activity – and employment – at which it does so.

From Glasgow to Ethiopia, from Toxteth to Cambodia, the world is crying out with desperate human need. To waste resources on the scale that (as we shall see) they have been wasted in a relatively prosperous Britain in recent years is hardly the moral basis on which 'Victorian values' were supposed to have been founded. But, just as I shall argue that this waste of the past few years has been both unnecessary and avoidable, I shall also argue that the fears of the man in the street about a 'Britain without oil' *need* not be realized if the appropriate economic policies are adopted. So much damage has been done to the industrial base of the British economy, however, that we may need the equivalent of post-war reconstruction without the galvanizing effect – one hopes – of a war.

I have explained elsewhere[2] how it came about that Britain suffered the recession of 1979–81, with all its damaging consequences for employment. For all the Government's claims that we have had a major recovery since then, it is stretching the English language to say that we have truly emerged from recession when we still have well over 3 million unemployed. Of the two factors principally responsible for the sharp rise in unemployment in recent years – the loss of international competitiveness (during the high exchange-rate period of 1979–81) and the continuing fiscal squeeze – it can reasonably be said that there has been some easing of the effects that these have had on the trend of output (which in 1983 and 1984 finally got back to the levels of 1979) but not nearly enough to offer a significant improvement in the general prospect for the unemployed.

Before examining these effects, however, it is worth trying to put recent experience into historical context. Monetarism, 'Thatcherism' and fiscal deflation do not account for all the ills of the British economy; nor did their imposition suddenly transform the economy's prospects from good to bad. It was a commonplace before 1979 that the British economy was in *relative* decline, in the sense that it was losing its share of world trade and was being overtaken by other countries in the economic league tables of output her head, standard of living and so on. But what happened after 1979, as we shall see, was a rapid acceleration of this phenomenon – the compression of perhaps twenty further years of relative decline into five, and all in spite of our possession of North Sea oil, which was supposed to give the country a big opportunity.

An interesting analysis of the deterioration in Britain's relative position as a manufacturing nation was made in November 1978 by Professor Wynne Godley, then Director of the Department of Applied Economics at Cambridge.[3] He pointed out that in the period 1963–78 the volume of exports of manufactured goods had increased at a rate of about 50 per cent every seven years but that the volume of *imports* of manufactures had risen by 100 per cent every seven years. (Godley had been issuing public warnings about the balance of payments trend since 1973.)

Britain had, of course, started the Industrial Revolution and had for a time been known as 'the workshop of the world'. As other countries industrialized in the nineteenth and twentieth centuries it was to be expected that Britain would become less pre-eminent. And, indeed, this happened. But what Godley drew attention to was the prospect of this nation, which depended so much on imported raw materials, becoming a net importer of manufactured goods if the trend of the 1960s and 1970s continued.

For a time the traditional surplus in trade in manufactures continued. Thus, Godley pointed out, it fluctuated around £5.5 billion during the nine years 1963–72, and there was 'no clear trend ... notwithstanding the fact that one series was rising so much faster than the other'. Why so? Godley explained: 'The reason for this is obvious as soon as it is pointed out; the balance was roughly constant because of the accident that, at the beginning of the period, the value of exports was rather more than twice as large, absolutely, as the value of imports.'

That 'accident' was a reflection of the fact that in 1963 Britain's trading position with the rest of the world was still in relatively good shape for all the erosion of market shares. And, as Godley argued, the adverse underlying trends were obscured for some years by the fact that the trade balance itself did not deteriorate – the trade balance being an item that always received close attention during those years. But the expansion of the economy under Edward Heath and Anthony Barber in 1973 produced a marked deterioration in the manufacturing trade surplus, which was restored by 1977 to its previous level (some £5.4 billion) only by what, at that stage was the biggest recession of demand and output since the war. This was brought on by the first oil crisis, which hit most countries. (GDP in the UK, having shot up 7.6 per cent in 1973, fell 0.9 per cent in 1974 and a further 0.9 per cent in 1975.)

Between 1977 and 1978 the volume of exports of manufactures rose by 6 per cent but that of imports by 16 per cent. The manufacturing trade surplus was now falling (to £3.9 billion in

1978), but this fall was being offset in the overall figures for trade by a £1 billion improvement in trade in oil – a harbinger of things to come, as the net contribution to the balance of payments mounted to £10 billion by 1985. Godley prophetically commented: 'Unfortunately, there are no obvious constraints in sight ... the important point is that the improvement to the trade balance provided by oil is nowhere near its peak yet; we can look forward to several more years of expansion. It will be possible to use this for some continued expansion of consumption, albeit at the cost of industrial depression.'

Britain was using the North Sea 'not to lay the foundations for regeneration of the economy' (a regeneration that Godley's diagnosis of the *trend* of the manufacturing balance indicated was needed) 'but to finance an expansion of imports to feed an essentially consumer boom. So far from regeneration the presumption must be that British industry is losing out fast to foreign competition.'

The subsequent deterioration was quite startling. Although the rising contribution from the North Sea meant that the Government could continually publish figures showing a balance of payments surplus on current account, the manufacturing trade balance was eroded so fast that by 1983 Britain had become a net importer of manufactured goods. Godley had talked about imports of manufactures rising twice as fast as exports *before* 1979. The Bank of England drew attention, in the autumn of 1984, to the fact that between 1980 and 1984 the volume of imports of manufactures had shot up by 40 per cent, but the volume of exports of manufactures had hardly changed at all. This was a graphic illustration of how, as a result of the combination of lost international competitiveness and domestic squeeze, many years further relative decline had been compressed into a few. Godley observed in the spring of 1985; 'Excluding North Sea Oil, the current balance of payments has deteriorated by £11.5 billion between 1981 and 1984: the balance of trade in manufactures, which had been in surplus – generally in very substantial surplus – throughout the previous two centuries, has been in deficit since 1983.'[4]

This brings us to the real threat posed by the prospect of the oil 'running out', or 'slowing down', or simply – as I have pointed out, this is most relevant – not continuing to increase its contribution. In the pre-oil days there were two principal constraints on economic policy-makers in Britain: one was inflation; the other was the balance of payments. The two were connected, in that if the rate of inflation became significantly higher in Britain than in competitor countries, then this showed up in higher domestic costs for British manufacturers, which in turn eroded their competitive position and eventually caused a balance of payments problem. Restrictive measures were then taken in order to protect the pound – or, more sensibly, the pound was devalued to allow the external value of the currency to come into line with the erosion that had taken place internally.

The big hope in the early 1970s was that, as oil production from the North Sea rose, the balance of payments position would be so enhanced that balance of payments crises would be things of the past. One or two politicians even indulged in the fantasy that whoever won the 1974 election would be in office for ever because they would have no economic crisis on their hands. This fantasy begged a number of questions. One was whether it was sufficient to deliver economic satisfaction in order to be in office indefinitely. Another was that if the balance of payments position improved, some other domestic problem would not turn up to cast a shadow across the economic landscape, such as an acceleration in the rate of inflation. A third was that there would be no external shock to the economy.

The rate of inflation did accelerate in the 1970s, and there were the two 'oil shocks' of 1974 and 1979/80, when the price of oil shot up, delivering a potentially crippling blow to the oil-importing countries. The acceleration in the inflation rate in the UK in

1974–5 – to a peak of 28 per cent per annum – aggravated, through its effect on industry's international competitiveness, the long-run deterioration in the export/import balance of manufactures referred to in the diagnosis by Godley. The first oil shock came when British oil had hardly begun to flow. Thus between 1973 and 1974 Britain suffered a sharp deterioration in its balance of payments figures, caused partly by the loss of competitiveness and partly by the quintupling of the cost of the oil imports that it, in common with every other oil-importing country, suddenly had to face.

British policy-makers began to recognize in 1975 that a fall in the exchange rate was required to restore lost competitiveness. This fall was slow to materialize, and when it did, in 1976, it arrived with a vengeance. The main policy issue was rapidly transformed from whether and how to engineer a small depreciation in the pound to how to rescue it from a 'free fall'.

What the Harold Wilson/James Callaghan administration of 1974–9 tried to do was to borrow its way through the first oil crisis on the security of all those North Sea oil flows that were to come. It made the correct 'Keynesian' diagnosis that the rise in the price of oil was the equivalent of a tax on the oil-consuming countries, levied by the oil exporters, or OPEC. Unless offset by expansionary measures, this tax would dig a hole in domestic demand. The British Government tried to conceptualize its diagnosis in the presentation of its balance of payments accounts by separating the 'oil deficit' from the rest and by arguing that it would be foolish for oil importers to try to eliminate this and cause needless deflation.

This approach ran up against a number of problems. One was that other leading industrial nations, notably West Germany and Japan, did not fully accept this diagnosis in the various international forums, such as meetings of the Organization for Economic Co-operation and Development (OECD), where such matters were regularly discussed. These nations, which were in any case recognized as good and efficient exporters, certainly took measures to expand their economies in 1974/75, but they also decided to trade their way out of the oil crisis and to eliminate their 'oil' balance of payments deficits.

The UK was therefore trying to do an unfashionable thing at a time when it was already in trouble anyway because of that loss of competitiveness. For a while the borrowing strategy seemed to succeed: special loans were arranged with Saudi Arabia and the Shah of Iran. (Some of these delegations went on bended knee, but in one case Harold Lever, the Prime Minister's special financial adviser, was greeted with open arms by the Shah, who was an old friend.)

For a time, too, Britain was helped by sheer inertia. The main oil exporters, such as Saudi Arabia, Iran and Nigeria, happened to be countries that traditionally held a large proportion of their funds in London. When these suddenly swelled, they certainly helped the Labour Government's financing policy. But when their investment advisers suggested a more sensible and more widespread diversion of these countries' portfolios, money began to flow out of London. It was the run-down of the sterling balances in 1976 that was the principal factor behind the sterling crisis of that year. And once it is the fashion to move out of a particular currency, that currency is in trouble, at least at its prevailing rate of exchange.

In due course Britain was forced to borrow from the International Monetary Fund (IMF) in 1976 and to arrange a special international loan through a consortium of banks. There was such universal concern about the British economy in 1976 that one major US bank refused to participate in this loan. But the confidence of the financial markets recovered fast after this, and before very long the problem was not a falling pound but a rising one, once more threatening British industry's competitiveness. One official involved in these negotiations commented: 'It was as if North Sea oil had suddenly been discovered on 1 January 1977.'

Being a prospective exporter of oil had not helped the UK much so far. How was the actual production of oil going to benefit the UK economy? The first, most obvious point was that in a world of energy shortage possession of oil was a benefit in itself. Even if the economy that possessed it was not a particularly dynamic one, it was surely better off than without it. In the country of the blind, the one-eyed man was king.

It could be argued that possession was not simply good in itself: it was particularly important, given the nature of energy. Energy is a fundamental natural resource, perhaps taken too much for granted in the economic analyses and discussions of the post-1945 world. It was a *sine qua non* of the Industrial Revolution and of all subsequent economic development. On the other hand, as Germany and Japan demonstrated after the two oil shocks, it is possible so to conduct your economic affairs, even during a period of oil shortage, that you make up on the swings (production of other resources) what you lose on the roundabouts (higher oil price). Because of its utility as a prime input into the economy, energy is also strategically important. This strategic issue figured prominently in discussions in Whitehall and Westminster during the 1970s over 'depletion policy', or how fast the resources of the North Sea should be used up. The potential boost to government revenues and the balance of payments pointed to a policy for exploration, development and depletion that would effect self-sufficiency as early as possible.

Any attempt to produce more than was needed for self-sufficiency would be open to the charge that the economic and security benefits of the North Sea for future generations were being threatened – simply because they implied that the oil would be used up too fast. On the other hand, as Stephen G. Hall and Fred Atkinson have pointed out, there would be dangers if the Government were too cautious in its depletion policy because 'oil companies will not engage in exploration and development without the incentive of future production.'[5]

Future generations do not have much voice in these matters. The position was to be reached where Nigel Lawson, by 1984, announced that oil production in 1983 had been 60 per cent higher than was needed for domestic consumption.[6] Were future generations being deliberately sacrificed to what had become the pre-eminent aim of government economic policy: as low a public-sector borrowing requirement (PSBR) as possible? Not exactly. Forecasts of oil demand by both the Government and the oil companies had proved much too ambitious in the light of the world recession and the conservation that followed the two oil shocks. This said, the Government's search for tax revenues did lead it into what Alex Salmond, Energy Economist of the Royal Bank of Scotland, described as a 'reckless production policy'.

A White Paper, *The Challenge of North Sea Oil*, was published in 1978. Stressing the windfall nature of North Sea oil – it was a temporary boost; it would eventually run out – it developed the theme that North Sea revenues should be invested for the future and not squandered. Its publication followed a detailed inter-departmental inquiry in Whitehall whose working title was BONSO (Benefits of North Sea Oil).

The White Paper took it for granted that during the years of oil production the capital base of the country would be built up. One of the main points examined was the suggestion that a special investment fund should be earmarked to see that the revenues were not squandered. In particular, it was thought, there could be investment in energy and power resources for the post-oil years. This proposal ran up against predictable departmental and political squabbling; the Treasury, for instance, was reluctant to 'hypothecate' a particular source of revenue, believing that funds from all sources should flow into the general pool and then be rechannelled through the Government's public expenditure decisions.

There was also the argument that one of the prime determinants of investment was demand and growth in the economy. If the extra revenues were simply allowed to flow through the economy and were not channelled off for something specific, then they would contribute to the general demand for goods and services and hence indirectly, through that route, to future investment. On the other hand, given the long-term deterioration in the country's trading balance, much of the boost might simply be swallowed up in higher imports.

There was already a portent in the country's experience with North Sea gas. Whereas there had been no flows of North Sea oil before 1976, North Sea gas had, as Adrian Hamilton pointed out in 1978,[7] been making a steadily increasing contribution to national income and the balance of payments for nearly a decade – the benefit to the balance of payments being £200 million in 1972, £1.2 billion in 1974, and £2.7 billion by 1977, or some 2.3 per cent of gross national product (GNP: the value of goods and services produced in the UK, plus income on investments held overseas).

But this steady build-up in the contribution from North Sea gas had hardly been noticed against the general background of the economic problems of the time. As one senior official commented: 'It has simply been lost, and that is what is likely to happen to the oil.' (It is worth recalling the trend, cited earlier, that had been pinpointed by Wynne Godley: the general balance of payments deteriorated in 1973–4 in spite of this contribution from gas.)

In fact, the flow of oil was going to be noticed and discussed much more than the contribution of gas had been. But its effects on the balance of payments, though larger, were for a long time to be swallowed up in a similar fashion and to receive little attention. Thus in 1980 and 1981, when the impact of the high exchange rate of the pound on British industry's competitiveness was at its most adverse, government propaganda was largely successful in arguing that exports were holding up well. In so far as they were 'holding up well', it was the total figure for exports that was doing so, including the rapidly rising contribution from North Sea oil. But it was remarkable how little serious questioning this kind of claim was subjected to at the time.

The 'exports are holding up well' argument was belied by those Bank of England figures citing a 40 per cent rise in the volume of imports and static exports of manufactures during the early 1980s. Another way of looking at it is provided by OECD figures comparing the performance of exports with the growth of export markets. In the three years 1981, 1982 and 1983, taken together, the UK's export markets grew by 6.8 per cent – that is to say, the countries to which the UK sends exports increased their volume of imports from all sources by that amount; but during the same three-year period the UK's shipments of manufactures to those countries actually *fell* by 5.9 per cent. West Germany's export markets grew by 5.3 per cent, but its shipments of manufactures to those markets rose by 7.8 per cent – that is to say, it more than kept up with world trade and in fact expanded its share.[8]

At this stage it may perhaps be useful to mention a fundamental point about exports. There is no particular virtue in exporting *per se*. The fundamental aim of economic policy is to increase a country's standard of living against a background of strategic safety. There may be differences of view between political parties over how to achieve an increase in the general standard of living and how to distribute the fruits – let alone over whether to redistribute the existing level of property and income. But differences over macro-economic policy usually boil down to differences of interpretation about how to achieve longer-term goals. The question 'Will a slight increase in the inflation rate harm such goals?', for instance, has been at the centre of the British economic policy debate for many years.

Exporting can be seen partly as one manifestation of Adam Smith's division of labour and of the principle of comparative advantage: that everybody stands to gain, both nationally and internationally, if people, companies and countries specialize in producing what they are relatively good at. But for a country as a whole, exporting is primarily the means of paying for the imports that citizens demand as part of their standard of living. The best way of appreciating this point may be to think of the hard-up citizens of the Eastern bloc: their countries are chronically short of 'hard currency' to pay for imports, with the proverbial consequence that the visitor to Moscow is offered a fortune for a Marks and Spencer sweater.

For many years after the Industrial Revolution Britain's external trade was actually in chronic surplus, which enabled – indeed, required – it to invest heavily abroad. In more recent times it has often been suggested that, although the visible trade surplus was falling, this decline was offset by a healthy surplus in so-called 'invisibles', or non-merchandise trade, a category that includes everything from investment earnings to the proceeds of tourism, insurance, banking and other financial services.

Behind the 'invisible' curtain, however, things were not as rosy as they were painted. While Professor Godley was pinpointing the erosion in our visible trade balance, there was a disturbing trend in invisibles too. Between 1970 and 1980, for instance, UK invisible earnings increased in volume by only 4 per cent, whereas those of our main competitors rose by 16 per cent.[9] The British Invisible Exports Council estimates that between 1972 and 1982 the UK's share of world invisible exports fell from 11.2 per cent to 7.7 per cent – a drop that was more pronounced than the decline in its share of visible trade.

It was somewhat ironic that among the sectors that were losing ground in the world's invisible stakes were those areas, such as the London Stock Exchange, that contained many a member who was only too ready to sound off about the erosion of British manufacturing industry's share of world markets, blaming the trade unions and so on. The figure that staggered the Bank of England in the early 1980s, and prompted it to stir up a 'financial revolution' in the City of London, was the one showing that, following the relaxation of exchange controls in 1979, 95 per cent of the investment outflow overseas was handled by non-British institutions.

Thus it is not necessarily a serious threat to economic well-being if a country's physical trading position is deteriorating, provided the effect is being offset elsewhere. There are many examples of countries, including Britain, that have managed to borrow their way out of a temporary crisis. But such borrowings are usually contingent on the prospect of a recovery in some sector of the accounts that is sufficient to restore general balance.

One can think of the British overseas trading position over the years as a series of potential problems, always eventually rescued by 'something turning up'. In recent years, with the trend of both manufacturing and invisible trade far from reassuring, that something has been North Sea oil. The present threat, quite simply, is that when the effect of North Sea oil is no longer dynamic, and if the other sectors go on deteriorating or not improving, then exports will not satisfy the desired level of imports, and the standard of living will suffer.

There is certainly very little evidence to suggest that Britain's desire for imports is anywhere near satiated. On the contrary, it seems to grow and grow, for perfectly understandable reasons. But if we pull all these strands together, we find some alarming trends. The Economics Department of Lloyds Bank, for instance, recently compared the position in 1984 with the prospect for 1990.

It found that the non-oil trade balance was in deficit to the tune of £10.7 billion in 1984 but that this was more than offset by a £3.1 billion surplus in invisibles and an £8.8 billion surplus in oil trade, giving a current balance of payments surplus of £1.2 billion. But by 1990 non-oil trade was likely to be in deficit by £19.3 billion, invisibles in surplus by £5 billion but oil trade only just about in balance. This pointed to a balance of payments deficit of £13.6 billion.

Things seldom work out exactly according to such forecasts: the implication is that, at some stage between now and then, the foreign-exchange markets may begin to anticipate such an eventuality, and the pound could fall sharply.

2 The Impact of Oil

We have seen that there was a deterioration in Britain's manufacturing trade before North Sea oil came on stream in 1978, before the Thatcher administration came into office in May 1979 and before the very rapid build-up in North Sea production in the early 1980s. Behind that build-up the competitive position of British industry continued to weaken, so that the manufacturing trade balance went from surplus to growing deficit, and forecasters such as Lloyds Bank projected a mounting deficit throughout the 1980s. How did this continued deterioration come about? Why did North Sea oil not magically transform the situation?

An important point to understand – and it may well come as a surprise – is that in one sense North Sea oil was not a great bonus at all. Before the two great oil-price rises of 1974 and 1979–80 oil was cheap and plentiful. It did not cost much, in terms of manufacturing output in the UK, to pay for all our imported oil needs. The combination of the price rises had the effect of forcing oil-consuming countries to generate a much higher output of manufactures for a given quantity of oil. Oil-consuming countries with no domestic oil production – such as West Germany, France and Japan – were therefore much worse off as a result of the oil-price rises. Britain possessed oil but had to devote considerable resources to extracting it from the North Sea – it did not simply gush out of the desert. As the Governor of the Bank of England pointed out in November 1980: 'We are fortunate in not having to expand the production of traded goods to pay for the same quantity of dearer oil, as other countries are having to do.'[1]

The Bank of England explained: 'North Sea oil and gas make the

UK better off than if it had been obliged, like most industrial countries, to import its oil' but 'the resources needed to produce a typical barrel of oil from the North Sea are large, and exceed those which were needed to buy it from abroad before the oil price rise of 1973.'[2] In other words, the combination of the price rises of the 1970s and the discovery of the North Sea reserves, said the Bank, 'leaves the UK worse off than if neither event had occurred ... the degree to which the UK is worse off is, however, small.' It would be a lot worse off if it had no oil; and those countries that have to import high priced oil *are* a lot worse off than they were before 1974.

The UK has, in fact, experience of both positions. Like West Germany and Japan, in 1974 it suffered an immediate loss of income and welfare, having to offer more manufactures per unit of imported oil. By the time of the second oil shock of 1979–80, when prices doubled, the UK was self-sufficient in oil. It did not therefore have to manufacture more goods in order to pay for the same quantity of oil across the foreign exchanges, but the resources it was devoting to the domestic production of oil were greater than were required to purchase oil from the Middle East before 1974.

As the Bank of England pointed out: 'In 1970–72 the UK devoted an average of less than 2 per cent of its GDP to producing goods for export in exchange for oil. In 1980 the proportion of GDP accounted for by real resources used in the production of oil and gas had grown substantially, to about 3 per cent.'[3] On the other hand, 'The percentage of GDP spent on oil in most developed countries without oil of their own has risen from some 1–2 per cent in 1970 to perhaps 6–8 per cent now – an increase in resource cost for such countries equivalent to 5–6 per cent of their total output.'[4]

But these figures take no account of the fact that the North Sea oil reserves have a finite life, the only question being at what point in the first half of the next century the oil actually runs out completely. At that stage the UK will have to find oil, or substitutes from somewhere, and pay for them. This prospect was in the minds of those who argued in the 1970s, without success, that some proportion of the North Sea revenues should be invested in energy production for the future, when their children or grandchildren would see a Britain without oil. This question was separate from, and more debatable than, our more pressing concerns. Should economic policy have been conducted as if the North Sea somehow made the decline of manufacturing inevitable? And should policy-makers not have been anticipating the time, in 1985, when the dynamic impact of the North Sea ceased?

The finding that the combination of oil developments at home and abroad had little net effect on Britain's economic welfare led the Bank of England to two interesting conclusions: first, that 'No spending bonanza is justified because of North Sea oil'; and, second, that 'No large degree of structural change [towards deindustrialization] is desirable or inevitable because of the direct effects of the UK's oil endowment.' Other countries would have to expand their industrial sectors in order to export more to pay for dearer oil. The UK would face that problem rather later – in the next century.

Clearly, the pattern of both production and consumption in the economy generally was bound to change in the face of dearer energy. Depending on the degree to which energy entered into their total costs, some industries, such as traditional heavy industries, would be affected more than others.

The first oil shock induced the beginnings of a general move towards energy conservation and less energy-intensive methods of production, but the long lead times in investment expenditure meant that the results did not show up for some years. The second oil shock ensured that any doubts there might have been about the need to adjust to a world of dearer energy were removed. The combination of the two events had an unmistakable impact. By the mid-1980s oil demand per unit of GDP in most industrial countries was well down (by something like one-fifth) by comparison with the period before the energy crisis. The old energy-intensive industries certainly suffered from this (they may have been energy-intensive either because they really needed it or because it was so cheap anyway), and new, less energy-intensive industries sprang up. This was a long-term, secular change in the pattern of demand and production. But by 1984, outside the USA, much of the world was in varying degrees of recession, so that demand for energy was lower than it might have been for 'cyclical' reasons too.

What was oddest, however, was the belief, which gained ground in the UK in the early 1980s, that somehow, as a consequence of possessing North Sea oil riches, the country *necessarily* had to *deindustrialize*. This belief was derived in part from an analysis of the economic effects of the North Sea made by two economists, P. J. Forsyth and J. A. Kay.[5] But it was also a convenient political rationalization, on the part of those most closely associated with economic policy at the time, of what was actually happening to British industry.

Arguments on the lines that manufacturing industry was bound to decline as a result of our possession of North Sea oil seemed to be pumped out of the Downing Street and Conservative Central Office publicity machines into ministerial speeches in 1980–81 as fast as the oil itself was being encouraged to flow. The line was: 'Stands to reason: if we're selling more oil, we're going to have to sell less of something else, aren't we?'

Since manufacturing industry *was* declining, and declining fast, such arguments had a certain appeal. It was reassuring to be told, or to tell oneself, that an unparalleled decline in manufacturing production and investment – the one down by 20 per cent in two years, the other by 40 per cent – was somehow ordained from on high, a manifestation of historical inevitability that Ministers were powerless to resist. This absolution also accorded with the oft-expressed view of Mrs Thatcher's circle that 'Governments can do nothing' or 'Governments can do little.'

The curious thing about this argument, and about the resigned attitudes it brought in its wake, was that even at a superficial level it did not bear much examination, and the closer one peered into it, the less examination it bore. There were many other industrialized countries, notably the USA itself, that possessed oil. The possession of oil in those countries had never been seen as in any way at odds with the fundamental belief that, as long as there were unsatisfied human wants and a desire for a higher standard of living, the growth of manufacturing output should at least not be discouraged.

Even in Holland, which was considered to be a test case of the effect that sudden riches from the North Sea can have on a country's economy, manufacturing output grew by something like one-third between 1970 and 1980. The popular theory was that Holland was suffering from the so-called 'Dutch disease' – North Sea gas revenues leading to a current surplus of the balance of payments, a high exchange rate, reduced international competitiveness and, thereby, deindustrialization. The Dutch exchange rate did rise during the 1970s, and older industries, such as textiles, were less able to compete in world markets; on the other hand, industries such as chemicals and electrical appliances grew rapidly, with the result that manufacturing output overall performed well – expanding, indeed, somewhat faster than manufacturing output in West Germany.[6]

The argument that British industry somehow had to contract because of the North Sea windfall was expressed sometimes in terms of output and sometimes in terms of the balance of payments, although these were related. In each case the analysis was curiously static, on the lines 'More of one thing means less of another.' Often there was a confusion between the 'relative effect' and the 'absolute effect'. Thus it is clear that if output of oil rises from zero to one-twentieth of GDP in rather a short time, then manufacturing output's relative position, its share of total output, will decline – unless, that is, manufacturing output itself suddenly spurts ahead, which it certainly did not in the period we are talking about.

Similarly, if the current account of the balance of payments is indeed in balance – that is to say, if manufacturing is in deficit by, say, £5 billion but service trade (including investment earnings from overseas) is in surplus by £5 billion – and if there is a sudden accretion of a £5 billion oil surplus, then something has to give if the payments position is to *remain* in balance. But the oil surplus does not necessarily have to be offset by a deficit in manufacturing. Much depends on the level of activity at which the economy is being run. If output equals 100, the current balance of payments 'surplus' is zero and there is spare capacity in the economy (that is to say, not all the factories and workforce are fully employed), then an expansion of demand and output from 100 to 105 is likely to reduce unemployment, bring in imports and induce a payments deficit. Oil production can then counteract this deficit. And if the economy is already fully employed (which, of course, it certainly was not in the period from 1979 onwards), then the oil boost to the current balance of payments may be offset if there is an increase in the flow of investment funds overseas. This will also have the effect of depressing the exchange rate. But, in any case, why should the current account have to balance? As John Flemming, Economic Adviser to the Governor of the Bank of England pointed out, a balance of payments surplus on oil could be counterbalanced by the accumulation of assets overseas, via the capital account, without any 'need' to move into deficit on manufacturing trade.[7]

Before we go further into this debate, it is worth disentangling two distinct aspects of the argument. It is by now fairly widely agreed that the sharp decline in output and employment in the UK between 1979 and 1981 was caused by a combination of two factors, acting like a pincer movement on British industry. One was the loss of international competitiveness resulting from a high exchange rate; the other was the tightness of the Government's policy – the 'fiscal squeeze' resulting from the Government's desire to keep public-sector borrowing as low as possible and to cut spending and raise taxes (or not to lower them) accordingly.

The fall in real demand and output of some 4 per cent between 1979 and 1981 constituted the biggest recession since the Second

World War. Demand in the British economy itself was depressed, and in the world economy as a whole – which was itself depressed but not nearly as much as was the UK – British manufacturers were competing on highly unequal terms. This latter point was illustrated by the over-valuation of the 'real exchange rate', a measurement that takes into account not only the sterling exchange rate to which we normally refer in everyday transactions (the so-called 'nominal' exchange rate) but also the effect of a more rapid rise in British export prices as a result of the wage and cost explosion of 1979–80.

The depressed state of the world economy affected all manufacturers, British and foreign. But the over-valuation of the real exchange rate was clearly a problem only for the British. It meant that British manufacturers were competing on worse terms both in overseas markets and in the domestic one. A superficial way of looking at it is to think of the Government's desire to reduce the PSBR as having been primarily responsible for the lack of investment and repair of the physical infrastructure of the economy – roads, railways, bridges, sewers and so on – and the over-valuation of the exchange rate as having its primary impact on the (internationally) traded goods sector. But the effects interacted: the private sector also suffered from a cut-back in orders from the public sector and from the effects of a tight fiscal policy in keeping demand generally low in the economy.

Probably the safest way to describe the squeeze of 1979–81 is to say that the high pound was one mechanism by which a generally tight policy affected the economy. But attempts have been made to separate the factors involved and to quantify their effects.

The National Institute of Economic and Social Research (NIESR) estimated in November 1981 that two-fifths of the fall in output in 1980 was attributable to the fiscal squeeze and one-third to the over-valuation of the exchange rate.[8] Hall and Atkinson,[9] using the economic models of both the NIESR and the London Business

School, find that the rise in the effective exchange rate (that is, the nominal average rate against all the leading currencies) of 25 per cent between 1978 and 1980 would alone have accounted for a fall in GDP of 2 per cent in 1980 and 1 per cent in 1981. (The total drop was 4 per cent in the two years combined.)[10] Artis and Bladen Hovell found that by 1982 output in the UK was 8 per cent below its longer-run trend; between half and two-thirds of this could be attributed to the combination of domestic policy, loss of competitiveness and world trade – 'and of these policy and the decline in competitiveness (mostly due, in turn, to policy) carry the lion's share of the explanation'.[11]

Because wages and costs rose so much faster in the UK than abroad, the 'real' exchange rate went up much more than the nominal one over this period. Dr Otmar Emminger, former President of the West German Bundesbank, told the Treasury Select Committee in October 1981: 'At its peak in February 1981 the real exchange rate was not only about 50 per cent above its depreciated value of 1976 but about 30 per cent higher than in 1972.' He added: 'This is by far the most excessive over-valuation which any major currency has experienced in recent monetary history ... the large real appreciation of sterling from 1979 to 1981 was probably the most important single element in that period's British economic policy, as concerns its effects both on domestic inflation as well as on British trade, production and unemployment.'[12]

The economic squeeze and the over-valuation of the exchange rate were connected not only by the fact that the latter constituted a squeeze in itself on industry but also in so far as high interest rates, themselves the results of the monetary policy, were in fact contributing to, or causing, the high exchange rate by attracting funds to London from around the world, thereby bidding up the value of sterling.

One must also distinguish between the degree to which the over-valuation of the exchange rate caused the decline, or the acceleration in the decline, of British industry over this period and the degree to which that over-valuation might itself have been caused by possession of North Sea oil. There was no obvious reason why British industry's base should suddenly contract because of North Sea oil. If anything, the question was whether some preparatory work on investment in new sources of energy was justified, or whether policy should be geared to an *expansion* of the industrial base in order to pay for future imports of energy.

The idiosyncratic idea that Britain needed to deindustrialize because of oil should not distract us from the fact that the higher price of energy did imply the need to adapt the industrial structure. Certain methods of production would have to be abandoned because they were too dependent on energy and therefore too costly, and the very process of energy conservation promised new opportunities of production and profit as manufacturing and service industries alike adapted to a world of higher energy costs.

Moreover, Britain was generally considered at the time to be undergoing a long process of 'relative' industrial decline. 'Deindustrialization' had been a vogue word for some time, quite independently of anything that might have been caused by the advent of North Sea oil. What this rather alarming term actually meant was that Britain was seen to be losing market shares, nationally and internationally, as a result of declining international competitiveness. (These points will come up in more detail in Chapter 3: we should remember here that, other things being given, one would have assumed a continuation of this relative decline after the advent of oil. Indeed, the Conservative Party in 1979 was so shocked at such casual assumptions about the continuation of this trend that it made an election issue of the need to reverse it. It was therefore even odder that within a year or so Ministers were telling us that a decline in manufacturing was an inevitable consequence of possession of North Sea oil wells.)

Whatever might be argued by apologists for the economic policies of recent years – such as that there had to be a transitional period before the phoenix of a new British economy could arise from the ashes – the statistics are clear: between 1979 and 1981 there was a sharp fall in manufacturing output, whereas in most other industrial countries there was a pause, in the wake of the second oil shock of 1979–80, before a continuation of the general upward trend in manufacturing output.[13]

At this stage it is worth recalling a Treasury-inspired argument that had a brief lifespan in 1980–81 but was, I suspect, never believed for one minute by the general public and eventually died of its own absurdity. This was the argument that Britain was not better off as a result of North Sea oil but was actually a lot worse off and, what was more, a lot worse off than other countries – even oil-importing countries such as West Germany.

The reasoning behind this view was that since it was clear that British industry was in a worse state than that of other industrial countries, Britain would probably have been better off without North Sea oil because the exchange rate would not have risen so high or caused such damage to manufacturing industry. This excuse offended the gut instinct of the common man, which was, fairly obviously, 'Without the oil where on earth would we be?' It also depended heavily on two (implicit) arguments: first, that the strength of the exchange rate was the inevitable result of North Sea oil and North Sea oil alone; second, that the reduction in manufacturing output allegedly caused by the (oil-induced) rise in sterling exceeded the value of North Sea oil output – a far-fetched assumption.

One way of considering the impact of the North Sea on the exchange rate is to think of the position of an oil-importing country such as France, West Germany or Japan. Other things being equal, in order to sell more goods to pay for dearer oil, such countries might benefit from a small devaluation of their currency. Devaluation in such circumstances discourages imports by making them more expensive and encourages exports by making them cheaper and/or more profitable. Conversely, it may be argued, a country suddenly endowed with oil might find its currency moving in the other direction as a necessary consequence of what was happening to the currencies of the oil importers.

But need such a move be very large? In examining the costs and benefits of such a currency appreciation, the Governor of the Bank of England, Gordon Richardson, pointed out in his Ashridge lecture (November 1980): 'The key question is whether nominal exchange rate appreciation is likely to involve comparable real appreciation or whether, as a result of compensating cost and price adjustments, the real exchange rate remains broadly stable in the long run. Because of repercussions on costs and prices, the effect of nominal appreciation in the exchange rate can be less than appears. How much less will, of course, be determined by the behaviour of inflation.'

We know what happened in the case of the UK. We had a huge rise in the nominal exchange rate, which, instead of being compensated by lower inflation, was accompanied by accelerating inflation. Between 1977 and 1980 – from a base a year later than that quoted by Emminger above – the nominal exchange rate rose by 25 per cent but the real exchange rate (because of higher unit labour costs) by 35 per cent.

If one imagined a manufacturer selling goods in the international market place for £1 at an exchange rate of $1.80, he was soon having to charge $2.25 for them in order to maintain his profit margin as a result of currency changes and $2.43 to allow for both currency changes and higher domestic inflation. The deleterious effect on the volume of sales if he maintained high prices is not difficult to imagine; the impact on his profit margin of not maintaining his prices also needs little imagination. No wonder the chairman of ICI went to 10 Downing Street in the autumn of 1980 and asked the Prime Minister whether she wanted Britain to remain in business.

The strange thing was that the belief in 1980 that the strength of sterling (its 'petro-currency' status) was entirely the result of

Sea oil coincided with a possible explanation that was closer to home and was pinpointed by the Swiss monetarist economist Professor Hans Niehans in a study commissioned by some of the Prime Minister's advisers – namely, the very high level of interest rates then obtainable in London by comparison with those in other investment centres.[14]

Niehans argued that interest rates were almost entirely responsible for the strength of sterling. Hall and Atkinson, too, argued that 'The primary responsibility for this rise was interest rate movements,' noting how sterling fell after the interest-rate policy was changed.[15] Only 10 per cent of the 35 per cent rise in the real exchange rate was attributable to the effect of oil, said Hall and Atkinson. Even the Treasury economists, who were at one stage expected by their Ministers to support the oil effect, put it no higher than 10 to 15 per cent.[16]

In evidence to the House of Lords Select Committee on Overseas Trade, John Flemming, Economic Adviser to the Governor, gave the Bank of England's view: 'Of a movement of about 40 per cent in sterling's competitiveness not more than a quarter could reasonably be attributed to North Sea oil.'[17]

Two other economists, Haache and Townend, managed to explain the pattern of interest rates and the real exchange rate over this period without having to introduce North Sea oil into their equations at all.[18] Another reason for being wary of the 'petro-currency' argument is that this was a period when the Government was acquiescing in a high exchange rate as a counter-inflationary weapon. This became clear to operators in the foreign exchange market who found themselves with a 'one-way bet' on a currency whose rise was not being seriously resisted by the Treasury and Bank of England.

As Hall and Atkinson point out, if it is difficult to quantify the exact impact of oil on the exchange rate,

the impact of the exchange rate on the rest of the economy is fortunately quite well understood ... as time passes the actual quantities of exports and imports will adjust to the new price relationships. That is, the demand for our exports will fall, due to their higher price in terms of foreign currency and the quantity of goods imported will rise due to the lower sterling price of imports. These effects will combine to produce a worsening of the current account of the balance of payments and an overall reduction in domestic production, due partly to a decline in exports and partly to imported goods being substituted for domestically produced goods.[19]

This sounds all very gentle in theoretical exposition. But we have seen how great the movement of the real exchange rate was and how drastic the impact on domestic production. A textbook might declare: 'These effects on output will tend to disappear as domestic prices adjust and the real rate of exchange eventually returns to its former level.' But the Morgan Guaranty index for the real exchange rate showed that in 1984 the UK real exchange rate had fallen by only some 10 per cent after that 35 per cent rise between 1977 and 1980.

Exchange-rate effects apart, the simple result of the production of North Sea oil on the balance of payments was, by the mid-1980s, very impressive. The gross value of North Sea output was some 5 per cent of the country's GDP, contributing over £20 billion a year to the balance of payments. Exports of oil accounted for one-fifth of Britain's total exports. At 2.5 million or 2.6 million barrels a day, the UK was ranked among the biggest of the OPEC group. By January 1985 the UK was producing the equivalent of more than one-fifth of total OPEC output. After allowance for imports of equipment directly related to North Sea output and related outflows of foreign interest, profits, dividends and capital, the net benefit was running at some £17 billion a year.[20] (The much quoted official figure showing a net contribution from oil of £7 billion to the balance of payments in 1984 and £10 billion in 1985 merely represented exports of oil net of imports. It did not include the figure of some £15 billion for UK domestic consumption of oil, which, of course, once had to be imported. Not having to import this was a major saving to the balance of payments.)

The position to which Nigel Lawson, the Chancellor, had referred, whereby the UK was producing 60 per cent more oil than its domestic requirements at this stage, was not entirely planned. The degree to which the combination of energy conservation and recession would reduce domestic British demand for oil (or keep it below what traditional relationships would have suggested) was certainly not expected.

The effect was to produce a 'hump' of oil, both in balance of payments terms and in terms of its contribution to the Exchequer. This hump occurred in the mid-1980s. Even on the most optimistic assumptions, production of, and revenue from, oil was due to fall from then on (the latter at a faster rate because later developments in the North Sea were allowed a more liberal tax regime).

The question arises: What would happen if the real exchange rate did not return to its former level but remained relatively high, thereby exacerbating the competitiveness problems of British industry? One possible scenario in 1985 was that the exchange rate would remain high for some years; that the erosion of the industrial base would continue; and that at some stage, perhaps in the late 1980s, perhaps in the 1990s, the gruesome pattern of the balance of payments developments outlined, for instance, by the Lloyds Bank economists would lead to a collapse of the exchange rate. This would eventually make British industry competitive again. But at what cost in terms of lost output and employment meanwhile? And just how large, or small, would be the manufacturing base that was at this stage given the chance to become competitive again? One thing is reasonably certain: capacity that has been eroded over a period of years cannot be rebuilt overnight.

The question 'What will happen when the oil begins to run out?' began to be more widely discussed in the course of 1984 and early in 1985. During the sterling crisis of January 1985, when the Bank of England had to reintroduce Minimum Lending Rate (MLR) at 12 per cent in order to stop a run on the pound, there were signs that the foreign-exchange markets might be beginning to anticipate events. After having praised the British economy, both for its stringent economic policies and for its possession of North Sea oil, foreign-exchange dealers – such as the head of foreign-exchange operations at the USA's big Chemical Bank – were quoted as saying, in a derisory context, that Britain was a 'one-commodity country'. That commodity was, of course, oil. And the parallels to be drawn were certainly with a kind of developing, or 'post-industrial', nation.

The case for encouraging an early adjustment of the exchange rate would seem strong. Yet after the January 1985 fall the Government went out of its way, through its policy of maintaining high interest rates, to keep the pound relatively high once again.

If a large adjustment to the exchange rate *were* to take place, then this would have obvious implications for the inflation rate. The very same exercise carried out by Hall and Atkinson on the Treasury, NIESR and London Business School economic models suggested that the appreciation in the exchange rate up to 1981 produced a price level some 8.5 per cent to 14.5 per cent lower than it would otherwise have been. In this sense, a fall in the exchange rate to its original level would bring with it not so much 'new' inflation as 'old' inflation that had been suppressed by the earlier appreciation. The eventual fall in the exchange rate would temporarily lower purchasing power and living standards via higher prices. But these would in turn have been temporarily boosted by the suppression of price rises earlier. And in the long run living standards depend on the growth of productive capacity, which requires a competitive exchange rate (among other things).

Some fall in the real exchange rate was predicted by Nigel Lawson in the speech he gave to a Cambridge Energy Conference in April 1984. This occasion was the first public signal that Treasury Ministers had changed their view about the 'inevitability' of the decline of manufacturing industry in Britain as a direct result of North Sea oil. The Chancellor was evidently anticipating market concern about 'Britain without oil' and emphasized that the decline in oil production – probably starting in 1985 – would not be a mirror image of the build-up since 1975. It would be much slower, he said, and the income from Britain's extra overseas investments – which were valued at £40 billion net in 1982, as opposed to £10 billion four years earlier – would help Britain's balance of payments as oil exports declined.

Several years earlier, however, the Governor of the Bank of England had pointed out in his Ashridge lecture: 'Overseas investment seems unlikely to match more than a modest part of the resources that might be required to safeguard our future position. Over the longer run we need to match a substantial part of the depletion of our oil reserves by investment at home.'

This was a very important point. There had been a time during the debate about the North Sea in the late 1970s when the Government, which had wanted to abolish exchange controls anyway, had partly justified this policy on the grounds that the outflow from London would offset the effects on the exchange rate of the pound's putative 'petro-currency' status. (This was before 1980, when the Government for a time acquiesced in the high exchange rate because of its counter-inflationary effects.) But, as we have already seen, the main explanation for the strength of the pound seemed to be tight fiscal and monetary policies. These brought high interest rates, which were attracting inflows of 'hot' money to London. If interest rates had been much lower, then it is very unlikely that the inflows of funds would have been so great, in which case a policy of offsetting them with outflows of long-term capital would have been more open to question. On the other hand, in each of the years 1980, 1981 and 1982 the UK had a bigger current-account balance of payments surplus than any other member country of the OECD (a cumulative £15.5 billion). The accumulation of foreign assets was one way of both not 'wasting' the oil and providing income for the future. But would the income be enough to offset losses elsewhere in the balance of payments accounts? And was investment abroad, however much it might fit a free-market model of the economy, a sufficient policy response when there was the threat to the industrial base, and to employment, at home? Running the economy at a higher level of activity would itself have brought in more imports, lowered the balance of payments surplus and the exchange rate and generally eased the pressure on industry and employment.

In his Cambridge speech Lawson approved the use of the oil revenues to bring down public-sector borrowing and said the reduction in the PSBR and inflation would ease the adjustment process as manufacturing industry rebuilt its trading strength. This seemed to be an acknowledgement that a resurgence of manufacturing *was* needed after all. The Chancellor added: 'It is reasonable to expect that there will be some return to the traditional trade pattern of a surplus in manufacturing and invisibles offsetting deficits in food, basic materials and, eventually, fuel.'

It was in this context that there would have to be a fall in the real exchange rate, Mr Lawson added. This did not necessarily involve a fall in the nominal exchange rate: 'The real exchange rate can also adjust by better productivity performance and greater restraint on pay.'

Such economic indices as were available by the end of 1984 suggested that any major improvement in the real exchange rate by such a route was still a long way off. Indeed, the Bank of England's December *Bulletin* found that, as measured by comparative unit costs, the British economy's performance had deteriorated again in the course of 1984 after some improvement in the previous two years.

The Chancellor assumed an improvement in Britain's forthcoming overseas trading performance and then said that obviously those sectors of the economy with a larger tradeable content would tend to expand in relation to others. Underlining his Government's

47

laissez-faire philosophy in these matters, he continued: 'Which industries and services they will be I do not know. It is not the job of Government to try to guess these matters. It is the job of industry and commerce. What is clear, however, is they will not be the same industries that many people attempted to persuade us to subsidize while oil production was building up.'

Thus in the principal policy statement made during 1984, in the face of growing concern about what Britain should do when the oil began to run out, the Chancellor of the Exchequer was in fact making a virtue of doing nothing and of leaving timing entirely to the market place. Faith was being placed in the British economy's assumed powers of self-regeneration, which powers were to manifest themselves in response to the Government's efforts to reduce the rate of inflation and to keep public-sector borrowing under control. These were the factors that were intended, way back in 1979, to help the economy to grow faster than its traditional rate of 2 to 3 per cent per annum, and they were the powers that were also, in the days of heavy recession in 1980–81, to lead to a self-sustained recovery, in which unemployment would fall.

Since GDP was only 4 per cent higher in 1984 than in 1979 – it had fallen and risen during the 1979–84 period – the average rate of growth was considerably lower than the pre-1979 rate. I have argued elsewhere[20] that this was because policy was almost entirely geared to fighting inflation – at the expense of real output and employment – and that although fighting inflation is a laudable objective, not only was there excessive emphasis on that objective, but also the wrong means were chosen in the attempt to achieve it.

The pace of wage inflation was certainly disturbing in 1979–80. Tolerating a high exchange rate – and the pound was still high against non-dollar currencies in mid-1985 – was one means of fighting inflation. But the evidence suggests that something like one-fifth of manufacturing capacity was lost in 1979–81 and that this was certainly not offset by a surge of new capacity.[21] To be critical of the Chancellor's *laissez-faire* approach is not necessarily to advocate *dirigisme* in economic policy. But simply waiting for the exchange rate to decline, in the face of falling North Sea oil revenues and a growing balance of payments deficit, while British industry remains uncompetitive internationally, seems an excessively passive approach.

3 Oil in Context

We have seen that energy in general, and oil in particular, had been taken for granted in economic policy for most of this century, except during wartime and its immediate aftermath. It was the two oil shocks of the 1970s that made people aware that this was a finite resource. Indeed, at the annual economic summit in Tokyo in 1979 a paper written by President Carter's Council of Economic Advisers (CEA) suggested that macro-economic policy might never be the same again and that oil had emerged as a major constraint on output, expansion and employment.

The second oil shock of 1979–80 was followed by a world recession, as the advanced industrial countries simultaneously took restrictive action in an attempt to counter the inflationary impact of higher oil prices and to cut their imports so that they could pay for dearer oil. As the 1980s progressed, it became clear that conservation was taking place in a big way. The USA, in particular, decontrolled energy prices and became less profligate and wasteful in its consumption. (President Carter had called this battle 'the moral equivalent of war').

The 1973–4 oil shock followed a period of rampant consumption by the industrial countries. Despite the anger directed towards the Arab producers who hoisted prices, the oil-price rises were an important signal. The 'doomwatch' predictions of the Club of Rome and the Massachusetts Institute of Technology in the early 1970s suggested that the industrial countries would simply run out of oil if they went on consuming it at the current rate. Higher prices were a signal from the market place – from the basic supply-and-demand laws of economics. The 1979–80 oil shock, however, occurred when conservation efforts were under way and the oil-consuming countries were only just recovering from the earlier shock.

The combination of conservation and recession arrested the seemingly inexorable rise in the price of oil in the 1980s; indeed, the story by the mid-1980s had become one of regular cliff-hangers at OPEC meetings focused on the question of whether the oil producers could continue to maintain price levels.

Looking back on the sequence of oil-price rises, it seems reasonable to deduce that, for all the criticism that was made of OPEC and the Arabs at the time, they were the messengers of economic history in 1973–4. Something, somewhere, would have had to give if we all went on consuming oil as if its supply were limitless.

And to judge from subsequent events in the oil market, notably the sharp fall in OPEC production and the easing of the price in the mid-1980s, the rise of 1979–80 might reasonably be taken to have had more to do with the disruptive intent of the Ayatollah Khomeini and the Iranian revolution than with signals from the laws of economics. It was directly triggered by Iranian action and exacerbated by panic stockbuilding, at a high rate (2 million barrels a day), among the twenty-three member nations of OECD. Accordingly, the price simply did not hold, particularly in real terms. On the other hand, it was certainly after the second oil shock that the conservation effort became most apparent. And, by definition, the recession of the early 1980s meant that the market for oil was not fully tested in buoyant world trading conditions. Nevertheless, the recovery of the US economy in 1983–4 was much more robust than one might have expected from the analysis presented by the CEA in 1979. If there was one thing that was not restraining the US economy at all in those years, it was oil.

Nor was oil a constraint on the UK. On the contrary: it was gushing out of the North Sea as fast as the Government could encourage it. But just as oil had been taken for granted for all those years before the 1970s, there was a curious sense in which the economy itself was taken for granted during the great monetarist/Keynesian and 'wet'/'dry' debates in the UK during the period 1979–84.

The debate became so heavily concentrated on events of the moment that there were times when it seemed that both monetarists and Keynesians thought that if only economic policies could be got right, everything else would follow. As a 'Keynesian' commentator throughout this period, I am well aware that my credentials for impartiality in this debate are necessarily suspect. Nevertheless, I should like to make an attempt to stand back from that debate somewhat and to put it in a longer-term context that is relevant to a Britain without oil or with declining oil revenues. This may involve an attempt at devil's advocacy – but not too much of one. The debate was so bitter at times, and the support for the Government so widespread in the press, that those of us on the other side had great difficulty in trying to be 'fair' because we regarded the ground rules as being rather weighted against us. One of the successes of 'Thatcherism', with its emphasis on devotion to the cause (Mrs Thatcher's frequent question was: 'Is he one of us?'), was that the critics themselves often felt cornered and isolated.

This said, the main worry of any 'Keynesian' in those debates was that there was always a danger of being accused of making things 'too simple by half' when putting forward various remedies – or not even remedies: merely criticisms of the way in which economic policy was being conducted. The Government was always able to make great play with the question 'What is the alternative?', which had great appeal to the layman. There is always an alternative. The question was silly but effective.

The alternative to making the problems of the British economy even worse was, amazing though it might seem, not to make them worse. One would not have made them worse by eschewing certain objectives and policies – such as a high exchange rate and an excessively restrictive fiscal policy – which hardly seemed designed to reverse the relative decline of British industry, let alone ensure that its resurgence, or its move into 'up-market products', would take place on a scale sufficient to make any difference to the country's fundamental economic problem.

For we all knew about that problem. It was perfectly consistent to argue that 'Thatcherism' or 'economic evangelicalism' was making matters worse without believing that there was an 'easy solution' to the longer-term problem.

However, the beauty of what the Thatcher administration was doing from the political point of view – and from the point of view of the many people who were concerned about the UK's economic problems without necessarily fully understanding them – was that it purported to offer a simple solution to these longer-term problems. While making them worse, in the eyes of 'Keynesians', it was in theory (its own theory) curing them. The pristine simplicity of it must certainly have appealed to the Government's publicity managers. As an indefatigable opponent of what the Government was doing, I have to admit that, in a perverse way, it even appealed to me. I admired its cheek.

The worries of traditional Keynesian economists about the British economy permeated the economic literature of the subject in the 1970s – and, for that matter, had done so in the 1960s and the 1950s. What much of that period demonstrated, though, was that in spite of those worries, the British economy did not perform too badly. It managed to stagger along, not growing as fast as the rest of Europe (certainly not as fast as Japan and the newly industrializing nations) but raising its citizens' standard of living year by year.

It was still possible to be convinced by the 'doom-and-gloom' school of British economics in the 1970s without leaving the country and then to go on a trip and decide that perhaps the fears were exaggerated. Thus, for all the worship of the Japanese economy that devotees of statistical analysis were inclined to indulge in, a brief trip to Japan itself was enough to put things into perspective.

When it came to the ultimate criterion, the standard of living in the widest sense, one could go to Japan in 1979 and, while being impressed by industrial efficiency, nevertheless note that the nation had been stung by the passing remark of an EEC Commissioner that it was 'a country of workaholics living in rabbit hutches'. Back in London one would be told by Japanese bankers that they much preferred Wimbledon Park to Tokyo, where they lived in sub-standard houses that, because of the intensity of their work and the distances they travelled, they seldom saw anyway. (I should not want to over-emphasize such 'anecdotal' evidence, but it cannot be entirely irrelevant.)

If there was a prevalent feeling about the British economy and way of life in the late 1970s, it was, I think, a belief that we had got away with it so far but that things could not go on quite as they were. The worry that relative decline might turn into absolute decline was not just anecdotal: it was widely transmitted in news-paper columns, in political speeches and even in the normally circumspect *Bank of England Quarterly Bulletin*.

So, in order to put the prospect of Britain without oil and the recent monetarist/Keynesian debate into perspective, it would be useful to go back to 1979 and to recall the debate that was going on then about 'deindustrialization', both in academic circles and in Whitehall, and through the medium of the National Economic Development Office and Council.

The deindustrialization problem was well highlighted in the epony-mous book edited by Frank Blackaby and published by the National Institute of Economic and Social Research in 1979.[1] Echoing the worries of Godley to which we have already referred, the conference whose proceedings were summarized in *Deindustrialization* agreed, in Blackaby's words, that 'The matter for concern was the progress-ive failure to achieve a sufficient surplus of exports over imports of manufactures to keep the economy in external balance at full employment' (services, or 'invisibles', not being sufficient to fill the gap). Or, as the Cambridge economist Ajit Singh put it: 'An efficient manufacturing sector for the UK economy may be defined as one which, given the normal levels of other components of the balance of payments, yields sufficient net exports [exports net of imports] (both currently, but more importantly, potentially) to pay for import requirements at socially acceptable levels of output, employment and the exchange rate.' Singh's phrase 'more importantly, potentially' was developed thus: 'For instance, a windfall gain to the balance of payments [for example, from North Sea oil] may put it temporarily into surplus (at desired levels of output and employment), although manufacturing industry may be incapable of ensuring this when "normal" conditions return.'

Sir Alec Cairncross, with his customary succinctness, commented: 'A contraction of industrial employment is a matter for concern if it jeopardizes our eventual power to pay for the imports we need,' and 'It is part of the "Cambridge" argument that, precisely because North Sea oil helps to close the gap in the balance of payments, deindustrialization will be allowed to continue for longer without check.'

The crux of the deindustrialization problem was put by these 'mainstream' British economists in 1979 as, not to put too fine a point upon it, the worst of all textbook worlds. Higher income in the UK produced an inordinate increase in the demand for imports, whereas higher income in the rest of the world did not lead to a corresponding increase in the desire for British goods.

Why was this? C. J. F. Brown and T. D. Sheriff seemed to summarize a thousand diagnoses when they said:

Non price characteristics such as low quality, late deliveries and poor design have been such that the demand for [UK manufactured goods] on world markets has remained low. These are consequences of supply difficulties, the more obvious examples of which include lack of mobility in the labour force, poor industrial relations, lack of technological innovation inability to respond effectively to, or indeed to anticipate, changes in the pattern of consumer demand, and inappropriate skills.

Those of us who were concerned about the way in which the exchange rate was allowed to rise from 1979 onwards did not dispute that there might well be something deep-seated about the British economic problem. Nor did we necessarily think that devaluation of the currency was a panacea. We did, however, think that if the economy was suffering from some or all of the familiar catalogue of woes, there was little point in making industry even *less* price-competitive than it was.

Similarly, while the tendency towards deindustrialization may have been apparent during the boom years of the 1950s, 1960s and early 1970s, we did not think that deflation, national or international, was going to make matters any easier. Most economic models – which are, after all, based only on what economists can derive from experience and observation – suggested that the prospect of expanding markets and general growth was a prerequisite of the new investment that alone could provide the jobs of the future. Depressing demand and multiplying the uncertainties facing business could hardly be expected to help, even though it was generally acknowledged that something needed to be done and that the country had to get to grips with its endemic problem of inflation.

It can reasonably be said that the kind of inhibiting factors on British economic performance listed above were commonplace complaints for many years before 1979. It is also true that such complaints can be made about the *average* performance of an economy and yet be perfectly consistent with the existence of good management, negligible union problems and impressive overall performance in certain sectors of the economy. It is probably also true that Britain has a comparative advantage in the way the press and television report labour and industrial troubles and that, for instance, first the docks and shipbuilding and later the motor industry, though their problems received 'saturation' coverage, were not necessarily typical or characteristic of the country at large.

But the trend identified by Godley and others includes all sectors: good, bad and average. It is the sum total with which they, and we, are concerned. And it so happens that sectors such as the motor industry, while not necessarily typical, were still very important, so that a deterioration in their trade balance could have a marked impact on the overall statistics.

The deindustrialization conference was somewhat inconclusive. While deteriorating trends in manufacturing employment and in the trade balance were duly noted, a sense of perspective was added by Blackaby's comment, 'Most participants concluded that this was an 1870 rather than a 1970 problem.' In Cairncross's words:

Let us accept that there is a stronger trend towards rising imports of manufactures than towards rising exports and that this bodes ill for the current balance. What follows? Is the situation any different from what it must have looked like in the 1870s, when rising imports of foodstuffs threatened the balance of payments and it was doubtful whether exports in the face of increasing competition from industrializing countries could pay the bill?

Sir Alec added:

At that time the adjustments were made first through the capital balance, which moved towards deficit, and later through increased emigration and improving terms of trade until world expansion pulled up exports again in the 1890s.

Yet the problem could in some ways be more formidable a hundred years later, Sir Alec suggested, because of entrenched social attitudes. As Sir Alec put it, in a passage that ought perhaps to have been studied more closely by the 'economic evangelicals' of the Thatcher administration:

If, for whatever reason, the United Kingdom has become a comparatively unpromising location for carrying on manufacturing, the adjustments required are not likely to be easy or agreeable or socially cohesive. They can, of course, be made to *appear* easy if all that is the matter is excessive government spending or unwillingness to limit the growth of imports. But what if the weaknesses on the side of supply are not within the control of the government, do not respond to protection of the domestic market, have little to do with the dynamics of market expansion and have their origin in ingrained attitudes or long-standing aptitudes?

Although worried about the trend of the economy and the manufacturing sector *before* 1979, the Keynesians, or at least some of them, were so appalled by the policies of 1979–81 that they may have appeared to put aside their deindustrialization worries in order to fight the bigger battle. One very good reason for doing this was that, as a result of the policies of 1979–81, vague longer-term worries about deindustrialization ('Is this an 1870 problem?') were superseded by stronger, short-term worries about what was actually happening to the real economy out there. For, by comparison with what had been happening to the manufacturing base and the trade balance in the 1970s, the following period produced manifest erosion of the industrial base and a concomitant sharp deterioration in the manufacturing trade balance. Thus, this was all really part of the same story. The fears were now being realized.

The decline in the industrial base was first denied by the Government, then rationalized. Exports were holding up well, we were told, when all that meant was that exports included a strongly rising oil contribution. The closure of factories did not matter because it was about time, was it not, that we got out of old-fashioned areas in which we could no longer compete? The fact that ICI feared it could not compete in the new areas at prevailing exchange rates, and lost 20 per cent of its UK customer base, was neither here nor there. Anyway, the government statistics were probably wrong: out there in the black economy, and in people's garages, the small businesses of the future were being formed, and these would provide employment ... There was a germ of truth in some of these rationalizations, but only a germ. Eventually even the Government had to admit that these were the best statistics we had, and there was no gainsaying them. Ministers then had recourse to the industrial miracle that would happen one day ...

So deindustrialization became a more obvious phenomenon. The 1979 conference had concluded with a classic demonstration of the 'two-handed economist' joke. On the one hand there were those who, as Blackaby summarized,

pointed out that we were already two-thirds of the way towards the likely maximum oil output, that we were a long way from full employment and that we still had only a marginal balance of payments surplus. Any projection into the future which assumed that UK exports would continue to move in relation to world trade in manufactures as in the past, and which also assumed that imports of manufactures rose in relation to home demand as in the past, produced either very slow growth rates and rising unemployment or very large and growing balance of payments deficits.

On the other hand some wondered whether exports were not getting better or were at least holding their own – the UK's share in exports of manufactures had not fallen significantly since 1973. And, while this was not true of the import propensity (Godley's main point), this was 'a supply-side problem, which supply-side improvements could alter'.

Despite this even-handed summary, the balance of opinion in *Deindustrialization* seemed to be on the side of growing concern. The suggestion that export shares had not fallen significantly since 1973 did not conceal the fact that they had fallen and that there had been a major devaluation in 1976 to restore competitiveness. And 1979 was followed, as we have seen, by a much more major *upvaluation* of the currency. The hoped-for improvements on the supply side were not, as it were, going to grow on trees, as Sir Alec Cairncross had made abundantly clear.

Which brings us back to the idea of taking the economy for granted. In the monetarist/Keynesian debate from 1979 onwards Keynesians tended to point out that there were ways of improving employment and output in the economy; that we knew them; and that these had worked for many years after the war. This view took for granted the assumption that the economy would respond, if not perfectly, as least in a more impressive way than it was performing under the new policies.

Were the projections on the lines quoted in *Deindustrialization* telling us that Keynesian policies no longer worked? I think not. They were certainly suggesting that such policies would be applied in a more difficult environment and might therefore be less efficacious than in their heyday. The experience of the 1970s had already demonstrated that. Yet there was a considerable difference between an unemployment level of 1.3 million in 1979 and the subsequent figures of well over 3 million.

The policies followed from 1979 onwards superimposed a demand squeeze on an economy that was already suffering from difficulties on the supply side. Experience had shown that a reasonable level of demand was a necessary but not a sufficient condition for attaining 'a manufacturing sector whose exports of manufactures were adequate to pay for full-employment imports'. To remove one of the necessary conditions was a strange way of going about the search for a sufficient solution.

Oil offered the Government the chance of a breathing space in the search for a solution to the supply-side problems that were apparent by 1979 but on whose gravity there was some disagreement. The tragedy is that the breathing space was not only wasted; it was used to make matters much worse and to turn potential problems into guaranteed ones.

What could have been done? We have seen that there were worries about the UK's ability to pursue economic growth and full employment without running into balance of payments difficulties *before 1979*. Although Singh had said a windfall like the North Sea might put the balance of payments temporarily into surplus at desired levels of output and employment, the operative word was 'may' – that is, assuming that high levels of output and employment *were* desired.

The UK's situation before the very rapid build-up of North Sea oil from 1978 to 1984 suggested that, given a relatively high pressure of demand in the economy, there might well be little worry over what to do about a large balance of payments surplus as a result of oil. (It will be recalled that it was such worries that led to the belief that manufacturing industry would have to contract to balance the accounts.) The economy could simply be run at a higher pressure of demand. This would involve lower interest rates and a smaller current-account balance of payments surplus – both of which would in turn keep the pound lower and (it seems reasonable to deduce) help to avoid the international competitiveness problem that had hit industry. There would then be more industrial capacity (fewer losses and more demand-induced new capacity) to meet the balance of payments problems accompanying a less dynamic oil sector. Professor Nicholas Kaldor put the point thus:

If countries plan for it, and use their new source of income, and particularly their additional foreign income, for stepping up the rate of capital accumulation to a sufficient degree, then it is perfectly consistent for other countries to pay for their imports of oil with exports of manufactured goods, without these exports impeding the development of the oil producers' own manufacturing sector.[2]

There were echoes of the Bank of England's view that the proceeds should go into investment in Kaldor's point that 'If the financial planning is so bold as to increase capital investment sufficiently to cause additional import demand to match the exports of oil, then oil will always be a blessing.' Kaldor's view was: 'To get this result, it must be deliberately planned: it won't happen by itself;

it won't happen as a result of the automatic operation of market forces.' Yet if the economy had been run at a sufficiently high level of activity, there is no reason to suppose that this result could not have been achieved. It was not market forces but government policy that kept activity down from 1979, hence dampening the inducement to invest.

In the early 1980s, of course, Britain did run a large balance of payments surplus, and the balance of payments disappeared from the headlines for a while, whereas for many years it had frequently dominated them. But the surplus was not an act of God.

The depressed state of the economy meant that, quite apart from the oil surplus, the balance of payments position was nowhere near the full-employment point that would have been the real test. The balance of payments position of an economy is crucially dependent on one question: At what level of capacity is the economy being run?

Dr Terry Barker, of Cambridge University, produced the kind of investment strategy that Lord Kaldor was commenting on. He summarized the 1981 government economic policy thus:

The monetarist policies pursued in the UK envisage the public-sector borrowing requirement being reduced by reductions in government expenditure accompanied by an increase in North Sea oil tax revenues. An essential component of the policies has been the appreciation of sterling, intended to reduce the rate of domestic inflation. The policies are leading to further deindustrialization of the economy.[3]

Barker looked at the trend of manufacturing output from 1957 to 1990, based on statistics published up to 1980 and projections based on the Government's announced policies. Between 1957 and 1973 he found a 'trend rise' in manufacturing's share in GDP, from 28 per cent to about 30 per cent. By 1980 manufacturing's share was down to 27 per cent; by 1985–90 it would be 23 per cent.

The steep drop in manufacturing production is apparently an effect of structural adjustment to oil production rather than the continuation of an earlier trend. However there is some evidence of more fundamental structural weakness in that manufacturing is falling more than oil and gas are rising . . . avoiding serious unemployment in this situation requires strong expansionary polices because the increasing energy exports employ very few people compared with the exports they are likely to replace.

As Barker pointed out, 'Manufacturing exporters not only employ people directly but they usually have strong linkages with other sectors.' He also emphasized the distinction between the kind of deindustrialization we discussed earlier and structural adjustment to oil and gas production. 'The Netherlands and Norway do not have the problem of deindustrialization as a fundamental economic weakness in that their estimated income elasticities for imports and exports are similar' – i.e., these countries do not have a chronic tendency towards balance of payments deficit.

The North Sea revenues provided an unprecedented opportunity to counteract the trend towards deindustrialization, said Barker. The balance of payments constraint – the manifestation of the deindustrialization problem – would be temporarily relaxed.

The low income elasticities of UK exports must be at least partly due to the use of obsolete capital equipment and restrictive labour practices associated with it . . . a major programme of industrial modernization and of both physical capital and working practices could take place against the background of the increased prosperity of the oil incomes.

But, so far from stimulating the economy through demand management, the Government from 1979 onwards did the reverse. As Barker commented:

Investment has been reduced not only because of the extremely poor prospects for the economy, but also because interest rates have been raised far above those in other industrialized economies . . . The British economy has undergone a recession comparable to that of 1929–31 . . . the profitability of manufacturing exports has been reduced and the manufacturing base contracted so that only the more profitable firms or those supported by government subsidy have remained in business. The depressed investment has tended to weaken even more the competitive base of manufacturing exports.

In advocating that 'the wasting North Sea oil asset ... be efficiently transformed into renewable physical capital on the British mainland', Barker suggested that, just as special government incentives were applied to North Sea oil exploration, so they could be applied to an investment strategy, with particular emphasis on investment in the regions. In fact, these regions suffered terribly after he wrote. There was, of course, no investment strategy at all: it was anathema to the Government's philosophy. But, again, such a *dirigiste* approach as Barker's would probably not have been necessary if the economy had been run at a higher level of activity, thereby offering more profitable investment opportunities to the market place generally.

The oil revenues were allocated, on the income side, to lower public-sector borrowing and, on the expenditure side, to higher unemployment benefits and consumption, much of which (because of deindustrialization) was spent on imports.

As Barker warned, once the oil revenues start declining, 'the traditional exporting sectors will have to start increasing exports sharply if huge balance of payments deficits are to be avoided at full employment. However, their ability to do this will have been eroded by years of decline.'

PART TWO

4 Britain's Fundamental Economic Problem

We have seen that possession of North Sea oil made Britain incrementally better off, during a decade of energy crisis, than countries such as France, Germany and Japan, which had to import oil. Because of the extra resource costs of extracting oil from beneath the sea, however, the oil was not so much a bonus as a well-timed compensatory gift, which meant that the UK was slightly worse off than in the 1960s, when it required only a small amount of manufactured exports to pay for imported oil. In other words, whereas the other countries were made worse off, relative to their recent past, the UK was made neither significantly better off nor significantly worse off. More important, because there was no obvious sign that wants were satiated, and because there were strong fears that we had a deep-seated balance of payments problem (deindustrialization), there was no good reason to suppose that possession of oil meant that we should acquiesce in a run-down of our manufacturing base – rather, that is, than in a switch to less energy-intensive production *within* manufacturing.

On the contrary: the oil offered Britain the leeway to do something about the deindustrialization threat. Production flows built up during the period 1978–85 to the point where oil was making a contribution of over £20 billion annually to the balance of payments and providing about one-tenth of the Exchequer's finances. The possibility of the North Sea windfall being devoted to an investment fund, or to the restructuring of manufacturing industry in some way, had been considered but rejected in the 1970s debate.

This was understandable, given the strong 'anti-*dirigiste*' strand in British public life. Indeed, it would be a brave man who claimed that he could have wisely invested a North Sea Fund. What is less understandable – or forgivable – is that demand and activity were deliberately held back on the one occasion in very many years when there was no obvious balance of payments problem in sight. It may be objected that there was a major inflation problem in 1979–80. There was. But instead of coming to grips with it, the new Thatcher administration severely exacerbated this.[1]

The North Sea simply got lost. During the period 1979–84, while the Keynesian/monetarist debate raged almost incessantly, the contribution from the North Sea built up fast, and the traditional trade surplus in manufactured goods disappeared completely. The one offset the losses of the other in the balance of payments accounts, and the rise in the Exchequer's take from the oil companies was absorbed – for all to see, or at least feel – in the rising cost of unemployment benefit. (This is not to complain about the paying of unemployment benefit. It is to take issue with the policies that allowed unemployment to rise so high in the first place.)

Between 1979 and 1984 the real level of output rose by 20 per cent in Japan, 10 per cent in the USA, 6 per cent in France, 4.3 per cent in West Germany and 3.9 per cent in the UK.[2] Over half the rise in the UK was the direct result of higher North Sea oil output, which rose from 1.8 per cent to 4 per cent of GDP.[3] Apart from that, the rise in output in the UK was a negligible 1 per cent or so. Indeed, output of the manufacturing sector alone was still some 10 per cent lower in 1984 than in 1979.[4]

One of the ironies of this period is that the opportunity of the North Sea was misused by the Government, whose leader made much of her 'sensible housekeeping' approach to economic policy. This was a Government that was dissatisfied with the traditional 2 to 3 per cent a year economic growth recorded in Britain and wished to accelerate it. But it ended up with the worst five-year period for economic growth in post-war history.

What happened during this period was that a severe cyclical recession was superimposed on a Britain that was thought to be in secular, albeit slow, relative economic decline but whose absolute levels of output had still been rising – by 3.1 per cent per annum in 1968–73 and by 1.4 per cent per annum in 1974–9, compared with average growth of 4.7 per cent and 2.7 per cent per annum in the Big Seven Western industrial countries (the USA, Japan, Germany, France, the UK, Italy and Canada) over the corresponding periods.[5] The policies that had been sold to the British public as the panacea for inflation and the secular problem – monetarism, a lower PSBR, etc. – produced a cyclical recession that compounded the long-term problem. These policies were fundamentally misconceived: they were based on a misunderstanding about the mechanism of economic growth and about what makes businessmen invest. Britain was a conservative economy, whose fundamental problem was a failure to change fast enough with the times and to produce sufficient quantities of what the changing preferences of consumers around the world, including those in the UK, desired. The Thatcher administration did not address this problem directly but focused on certain aspects of Britain's economic conservatism, such as the trade unions, and certain aspects of the economy that it found undesirable, such as the size of the public sector, and attacked these. And yet by 1985, even after all the sacrifices the economy had made, unit labour costs were rising faster than those of the UK's major competitors, so that it was debatable whether the Government had made long-term gains on the union/wages front.

It was always open to the Government to consider that such problems as union restrictive practices were symptoms of a deeper British malaise, but they were assumed from the start to be a (probably *the*) fundamental cause of Britain's relatively poor economic performance. Similarly, the size of the public sector was asserted, and *assumed*, to be economically bad in itself; it was further assumed that, provided this could be contained, somehow or other an economic miracle would result. These assumptions seemed to stretch to the belief that transferring the ownership of monopolies such as British Telecom from the public *qua* taxpayers to the public *qua* shareholders would somehow improve their efficiency.

Some comparative OECD statistics, covering the period before and during the rapid build-up of North Sea oil production, put Britain's manufacturing performance into perspective. Between 1973 and 1979 real value-added (or net) output in manufacturing rose by 5.1 per cent a year in Japan, 2.0 per cent in the USA, 1.8 per cent in West Germany and 2.9 per cent in France. In the UK, however, it fell by an average of 0.7 per cent a year.

These statistics are interesting because they throw light on some of the shadier areas of the 'debate' about manufacturing trends that led to such glib statements as 'Britain is no exception; all countries are deindustrializing.' Plainly they were not in the 1970s, even though the pace of manufacturing expansion was slower than in the 1960s. Equally plainly, the UK's performance, even before 1979, was disturbing. The comparative figures certainly show that there were grounds for concern that Britain was not performing as well as its neighbours.

What about services? Many a politician has sought comfort in the belief that, even if the UK was not doing very well in manufacturing, it was streets ahead in the provision of services, what with the City of London and so on. Again, the comparative statistics simply do not bear this out. Between 1973 and 1979 real value-added output in services grew by 3.6 per cent a year in Japan, 3.3 per cent in the USA, 3.8 per cent in France, 3.2 per cent in West Germany and 2.0 per cent in the UK.

As we saw earlier, the UK's invisible earnings from foreign trade in services increased in volume by 4 per cent between 1970 and 1980, whereas those of our main competitors rose by 16 per cent.

After 1979, of course, there was a world recession induced partly by the second oil shock and partly by the policy reaction to it. In Japan the period 1979–82 nevertheless saw real value added in manufacturing rising by 8.3 per cent a year. In the USA it fell by

2.8 per cent a year; in France the fall averaged 0.3 per cent a year and in West Germany 1.4 per cent a year. In the UK the fall was a staggering 5.0 per cent a year ...

So where does the British manufacturing sector stand after the combination of the secular problems that became increasingly apparent in the 1970s (the average fall of 0.7 per cent a year in manufacturing value added in 1973–9 compared with an average rise of 3.0 per cent a year in 1960–68 and of 2.9 per cent a year in 1968–73) and the severe recession of 1979–82?

A very interesting assessment was made by the National Economic Development Office (NEDO) in 1984 for the National Economic Development Council (NEDC). NEDO is the permanent staff that services the monthly meetings of the Council, at which Ministers, industrialists and trade union leaders traditionally sit around the same table to discuss economic and industrial questions.

The NEDO work draws on the reflections of economists both within and outside Whitehall. A memorandum presented by the then Director General, Sir Geoffrey Chandler, was at first marked 'restricted' and then deemed fit for general circulation. It seemed to me to succeed in standing above the various acrimonious debates about the economy at the time and to tell the story 'as it was'.[6]

Before summarizing its conclusions, I should like to make some basic points about the British economic problem as I see it – points that I hope will be helpful in interpreting the NEDO paper. One often hears people expounding their pet theories about what is wrong with the British economy: management, the unions, the Government, failure to adjust to the End of Empire, the class (and educational) system and so on. One frequently hears, in this context, that suggestions that British industry needs to be more competitive (through a lower exchange rate or less cost inflation) are beside the point because the real problems of the UK economy are the non-price factors, such as delivery dates, quality of product and so on.

Such points were aired, for instance, in the deindustrialization debate we discussed in Chapter 3.

The boring possibility is that these explanations may not be mutually exclusive at all – though recognition of this possibility makes for less heated pub and dinner conversation. There may be *something* in *all* these explanations, or they may themselves be part of a more deep-seated and fundamental cause, as I have hinted. But unless we get to grips with the relevant problem, we stand little chance of addressing the solution.

For example: I referred in an earlier chapter to the competitiveness point. One may have considerable sympathy with people who have a distaste for devaluation of the currency. But if, as happened in the UK in 1979–81, the domestic inflation rate is much higher than that of competitor countries, then – other things being equal, and whatever the truth about delivery dates and so on – that very experience is going to make the competitiveness position worse. And if, instead of reflecting the internal depreciation of the currency by falling, the exchange rate is actually allowed (even encouraged) to rise, then the problem will become even worse. At some stage a correction will be in order simply to get the competitive position of the country's industry back to square one. The fact that square one was not a very happy position either is no excuse for actions that simply drive the players off the board. Concern for the exchange-rate aspect need not drive out concern for other, perhaps more fundamental, aspects of competitiveness.

Again: all possible attention may be paid to various aspects of an efficiency drive within a firm or industry, but if the prevailing atmosphere in domestic or world markets is one of recession and lack of growth prospects, then the effort may come to little. A thriving market and opportunities for expansion would seem to be a *sine qua non* of the incentive for profitable investment plans.

This said, let us look at the impartial analysis of British industry's problems delivered by the Director General of NEDO in 1984. Its essential message was this:

Relative rates of innovation play a major part in determining the trade performance of advanced industrial countries (AICs). Capital investment plays a subsidiary role; comparative advantage in capital-intensive mass production of standardized commodities has shifted to the Newly Industrializing Countries (NICs). There is evidence that the UK's rate of innovation has been falling behind that of its principal competitors and that whilst investment in manufacturing continued to grow during the 1970s, a sizeable proportion of it was allocated to defensive cost-saving investment rather than to expansionary investment in support of innovation.

This gentle bureaucratic wording led up to a worrying conclusion, although, once again, it was almost thrown away in the wording:

Consequently it appears that the UK now enjoys [sic] an intermediate status between the AICs and NICs and has features of both types of economy in trade with the other. There are also indications that the competitive structure of UK trade has been moving towards capital-intensive and away from knowledge-intensive types of production.

Behind a welter of statistical analysis and comparison the NEDO study paints a picture that is both disturbing and comforting – comforting only in the sense that what it tells us does not really come as a surprise but fits in with the general anecdotal picture that most people probably already have of the British economy.

The picture is not one in which there are obvious villains. NEDC contains both industrialists and trade union leaders as well as Government representatives; it does not point the finger at unions or employers or the Government. Whether one blames poor management, recalcitrant unions or unhelpful or interfering Governments is neither here nor there at this stage. What is crystal-clear is that the general combination produces a consuming public that certainly wants to share in what the world's producers can offer but a British industry that is slow to adapt.

The NEDO study fills in the details of the kinds of trend that Wynne Godley has warned about. In the 1970s the main criterion appeared to be increasing import penetration rather than loss of export share. But by the 1980s (as we have already seen from OECD data quoted earlier) it was both.

The layman's impression that not all is bad (and what about such good companies as ICI?) is borne out by the statistics.

The evidence from export shares [of the combined exports, that is, of the Big Six OECD countries, the USA, West Germany, Japan, France, Italy and the UK] suggests that the pattern of UK competitiveness is biased in favour of two broad sectors, chemicals and food, drink and tobacco, where UK export market shares are some 1.5 per cent to 2 per cent above the manufacturing average of 12.4 per cent, and against the metal manufacturing and engineering industries, where export market shares are generally well below the average.

These biases are not new. The NEDO paper pointed out that developments in the course of the 1970s had reinforced them.

In betweeen are what NEDO calls the 'traditional' industries, such as textiles, timber products and clay, glass and rubber and leather products. These were closer to the OECD average, and in some cases above, although, being standardized products that compete mainly on price, they were badly hit by the rise in the pound after 1979.

The study took overseas trade balances in the various sectors as a percentage of home demand, in order to establish international comparisons that allowed for changes in both import penetration and shares of export markets: 'The major weakness in the UK's competitive structure once again centres on the engineering sector where the surplus, at 6 per cent of home demand, was considerably smaller than the surpluses in the same sectors of France, West Germany and Japan, which stood at 10 per cent, 33 per cent and 26 per cent respectively of their home markets.'

The problem with weakness in the engineering sector was that this accounted for some 40 per cent of manufactured exports. It was thus a very major weakness for an industrial country. The fact that the UK was average or above average – in relation to other

OECD countries – in traditional industries and weak in engineering and metal manufacture meant, said NEDO, that 'the UK suffers from a lower degree of trade specialization along the lines associated with advanced industrial economies.' NEDO also pointed out: 'Third World competition has not made more serious inroads into the UK market than in other countries, neither at the overall manufacturing level nor in individual industries. The predominant origin of increased penetration has been from imports from other OECD countries.'

The conservatism highlighted by the report, the sluggishness of Britain's adaptation to a changing world, comes out where one would, on reflection, expect it to: new products and new methods of production are closely associated with research, development and the patenting process. In all these NEDO found Britain lagging behind.

Technological leads and lags are – again, not surprisingly – associated with the various competitiveness indicators that tend to be quoted. If a country is speedy enough and adaptable enough, it can stay one step ahead: 'Divergences in costs arising from different wage levels, raw material costs, etc., can in principle be offset by differences in the efficiency of the manufacturing process – or bypassed in the development of new, sophisticated products, the demand for which is insensitive to price.' But if a country does not stay one step ahead ...

There is a considerable difference between the roles of 'innovation through the adoption of new products and *novel* processes' and of 'lowering unit labour costs in the production of established products by substituting "conventional" capital equipment for labour'.

A study of G. Dosi and L. Soete[7] found that levels of patenting play a strong positive role in export performance and that new investment is most effective when it complements a firm's innovative activities. This study also probably fitted in with the layman's instinctive feeling about international competitiveness in finding that technology gaps were more influential than costs in determining changing competitiveness between countries.

What the NEDO look at the position of British industry at the end of the 1970s certainly did not suggest was that there was any justification for a wholesale retreat from the traditional industries. More modern methods, more research, a shake-up in product development and marketing – by all means. But the idea that the UK was sustaining a lot of industries that we should simply 'get out of' – an idea often aired by Ministers during the early 1980s in order to rationalize what was going on – was never seriously suggested.

The fact that demand was then depressed at home, and that the exchange rate was allowed to price large sections of industry out of business, fits in with the view that many years of gentle, relative decline were suddenly compressed into a few in the early 1980s. Nevertheless, NEDO, quoting Katrak,[8] noted that during the 1970s there had been a trend for UK production technology to become more capital-intensive and less technology-intensive – i.e., labour- and cost-saving but not innovative. These developments were unfavourable in the long term because 'mature products, i.e., capital- rather than knowledge-intensive products, are likely to face a larger range of competing substitutes than would new products, and hence command lower returns per unit of input.' NEDO added the ominous thought: 'The developments may also make the achievement of full employment more difficult if, as past trends suggest, world trade in mature products grows more slowly than for more advanced products.'

NEDO studies of trends during the 1970s confirmed Katrak's thesis:

The key role played by the UK's weakness in product innovation is demonstrated by the association between changes in UK export market shares and changes in patent shares (the UK's share of patents taken out in the USA by firms of foreign origin) across twelve sectors, including all the major research-intensive sectors. This clearly shows the weakness of

UK engineering sectors in both innovation and export performance – and the better performance of the chemicals sector.

As NEDO added, while this correlation did not of itself establish the direction of causalty, 'the chance that it runs from better export performance to greater patenting activity is remote, given that patent protection is sought immediately the new products are introduced to a market – or even in advance.' (The chairman of ICI, Mr John Harvey-Jones, told me in March 1985 that the pace of innovation was now so rapid – 'When the need is identified, we can more or less arrange the invention' – that the registering of patents was no longer a reliable guide. This does not, of course, rule out the fear that some of the non-ICIs of this world who were slow at patenting in the past may, as it were, be equally sluggish at *not* patenting.)

Although the NEDO study was produced in 1984, the problems and time lags involved in assembling the appropriate international data at what is known as a 'disaggregated' level mean that much of the statistical work does not go beyond 1981. Yet the OECD figures at the macro level quoted earlier show a dramatic loss of our share of manufactured exports in the subsequent years. Taken with the 40 per cent rise in imports of manufactures between 1979 and 1983–4 spotlighted by the Bank of England, the loss of export shares does not make the movement into balance of payments deficit in manufacturing during 1983 particularly surprising. (The manufacturing trade deficit was £5.5 billion in 1983 and £7.5 billion in 1984.)

Does this manufacturing deterioration matter if, as we are often told, services make up the difference? The problem is that they do not. The UK's share of world traded services fell from 11.2 per cent in 1972 to 7.7 per cent in 1982, and its invisibles balance of payments surplus actually fell in real terms over the period.[9] In any case, services and manufacturing are not necessarily substitutes for one another. They are often closely linked. Indeed, as the NEDO study pointed out:

Several important industries, including the utilities, construction, transport, insurance and banking, are dependent on manufacturing for a substantial proportion of their business. A major determinant of the competitiveness of export services is the efficiency of the manufactured inputs required, particularly where close technical collaboration is necessary. All the more successful industrial economies have exhibited rapid growth of manufactured exports.

The fact that trade in services, as well as manufacturing, has not been doing very well internationally should give pause for thought among those who glibly assume that they will take up the slack. Taken with the virtual certainty that the balance of payments contribution from the North Sea peaked in 1984–5 and that the only question is the slope of the decline, it is not surprising that both the Chancellor[10] and NEDO point to the need for a return to overseas trade surplus in manufactured goods if living standards are to be maintained.

One conclusion that emerges with reasonable clarity from the analysis so far is the implication that, to make up for the erosion of the manufacturing trade surplus, a large fall in the exchange rate is required. This is what simple theory tells us if the export/import trend is unsustainable. It also tells us that such a decline is at some stage likely to be set off by the market place anyway, whatever might be the views of the Government concerned.

As the NEDO study put it: 'Faster expansion of manufacturing is to be expected when, in time, the exchange rate reflects the decline in oil revenue.' But here there are problems, and the process may not be symmetrical – that is to say, the sharpness with which exports and industrial capacity were lost when the exchange rate was allowed to rise in 1979–81 may not be followed by a smooth transition. For one thing, much capacity has been lost for ever. For another, because of companies' need for retrenchment and their desire to restore their financial position, there has been little in the way of long-term planning for an upsurge that might occur if the exchange rate should fall. As Lord Kaldor remarked in November 1984: 'Despite all the talk about developing new industries, manufacturing investment is still 30 per cent down in volume [on 1979].'[11] Again, as the NEDO study pointed out:

A main determinant of successful industrial expansion is the past record of companies concerned. This determines (1) the profits available for innovation and expansion, (2) the state of the balance sheet upon which the ability to raise funds is heavily based, (3) the amount of research and development upon which future competitiveness heavily depends and (4) the extent to which companies have ensured a programme of products, each with a life-cycle that is phased to fit with the rest of its programme and which together provide, at any one time, a balanced portfolio of new and established products, high-risk and low-risk ones, cash-generating and cash-absorbing ones.

Given these considerations, after six or seven years of relative economic weakness a lower exchange rate, while an important and necessary condition, might well not be sufficient to produce a rapid expansion of manufacturing, the NEDO study warned. Moreover, the UK would be attempting to bring about a 'structural adjustment' in the face of competition from countries that had already achieved this or were well on the way to doing so.

During the early 1980s the Government made much of alleged improvements in productivity. The figures available from OECD comparisons suggest that the improvements were never as great as Ministers seemed to imagine, by comparison either with previous UK performance or with the experience of other countries. But what studies by both NEDO and Christopher Freeman and Luc Soete at OECD brought out was how misleading statistics about improvements in output per man could be.[12] Another study, by L. Mendis and J. Muellbauer, emphasized that the improvements in productivity in 1979–80 in the UK were essentially a short-term phenomenon, depending heavily on the scrapping of the least good equipment.[13]

A number of economists had pointed out that improvements in productivity when output was falling were a bit like an attempt to improve a cricket team's batting average by using only the seven or eight best players: the average might be higher, but the score would be lower. Freeman and others drew attention to the crucial, and basic, distinction between 'capital-deepening' and 'capital-widening'. Capital-deepening, by substituting machines for labour, might raise labour productivity, but it did not necessarily do much for capital productivity, or total output, or the future prospects for total output. Capital-widening, however, and the further development of products and markets, offered the prospect of output, productivity and employment rising simultaneously. In economic growth, capital and labour do not have to be regarded as substitutes: they are complementary parts of the process. Of all the big industrial countries, Freeman and Soete wrote:

The United Kingdom seems to be confronted with the severest capital-shortage problems. In order to maintain employment at its present level ... an average output growth of 3.5 per cent is required ... in the short to medium term (1981–90), the required [manufacturing] investment growth is ... 15.5 per cent a year, which corresponds to an average level of investment [of £5.4 billion] well above the highest investment level ever achieved in the UK [£3.3 billion in 1979, both figures in 1975 prices].[14]

What the NEDO analysis of the prospect for British industry was drawing attention to was this: with manufacturing investment relatively depressed – and much of the investment taking place being defensive, in the sense of substituting capital for labour rather than being innovative – industry was not going to be in the best shape to take anything like full advantage of a fall in the exchange rate, which would be the manifest and inevitable result of the move into balance of payments deficit portended by the existing trend.

Given the association between research and development expenditure, new patents and exporting success, the conclusion of the NEDO analysis was that the UK should be putting resources into research and development in order to pave the way for the transition towards a greater manufacturing effort when the North Sea revenues begin to run down. (Engineering, needless to say, seemed in the early 1980s to come out badly in international comparisons of relative expenditure on research and development.) It did not explicitly make the connection that running the economy at a higher level of activity, and putting the emphasis of policy on real expansion rather than on the reduction of public-sector borrowing, might have improved the prospects for research, development and profitable investment in the UK. NEDO wrily commented: 'While a shift back from oil to manufacturing is certainly likely to help in terms of numbers of jobs, a continuation of the trends described in this paper and the factors underlying them would limit new job opportunities.'

To recap: the trends were, first, an emphasis on job-replacing investment rather than on investment for innovation and expansion; second, the UK's comparatively heavy dependence on product areas facing intense and growing competition from the newly industrializing countries; and third – implied by these trends – lower growth of demand elsewhere in the economy because of the sluggishness of the export sector (given the interdependence between manufacturing and the services). It goes almost without saying that, given the emphasis that NEDO placed on research and development spending, in the 1984 comparison the UK came way down the line in relation to other OECD countries.

One of the themes of this book is that it would have been less wasteful to the economy to have pursued, throughout the 1979–85 period, a policy towards the exchange rate that aimed at maintaining the UK's international competitiveness and anticipating the end of the dynamic contribution of the North Sea to the balance of payments (on current account). It will obviously take time, when the exchange rate does adjust, for British industry to adapt to the new situation, but the NEDO study concluded by being even gloomier than the present author: 'The exchange rate certainly cannot by itself be relied upon to generate the growth of manufacturing required. Having its main impact on price rather than non-price competitiveness, it will make less difference to the UK's competition with other OECD countries for high value-added products where our performance has been relatively worrying.'

Lower labour cost increases were one prerequisite of industrial recovery, according to NEDO. Apart from improving competitiveness, they would leave more funds for capital and innovative investment. But if lower labour costs were seen as the only route to industrial recovery, then the UK would remain over-dependent on lower value-added and price-sensitive products: 'Lower real earnings than otherwise would be the price paid for insufficient expansion of higher value added and more innovation-intensive products.'

NEDO's solution to the problems of adjustment to the tailing off of North Sea oil revenues became 'to help maintain and expand the design and development side of manufacturing during the period of exchange-rate pressure'. NEDO echoed a Confederation of British Industry (CBI) plea for improvements in design, production, engineering and managerial and marketing practices: 'This probably represents the only route available to the UK to become a high-income, high-growth economy as the contribution of North Sea oil declines.'

Investment in these areas was, concluded NEDO, the appropriate channel for North Sea oil money. 'It therefore seems highly desirable that a greater proportion than at present of the income derived from North Sea oil should be channelled to this end rather than to consumption, unpalatable as this conclusion may be.'

I have examined and explained the NEDO study at some length, partly because of its intrinsic relevance to the subject of this book, partly because it was one of the few detailed exercises on the subject to have been conducted in recent years. We are talking, after all, of a period when the Government in office professed, for a long time, not to believe in the need for an industrial policy or for government intervention in general, let alone extra public funds for research and development. Indeed, one of the features of the public-expenditure exercises of the early 1980s was the regular cut in government spending on industry and training, although in the end the Government, like its predecessor, found itself doling out large funds for companies, such as BL, that it regarded as lame ducks. NEDO itself, incidentally, survived as an institution only by the skin of its teeth.

It is not exactly reassuring that much of the evidence on which the NEDO study was based came from a period (the 1970s) when the general atmosphere was one of economic growth – or at least of more economic growth than in the 1980s. The investment and expenditure on research, development and marketing that NEDO called for to facilitate adaptation to the decline in the oil revenues is the kind of spending that is normally associated with rising demand and the expectation that demand will continue to rise. Most studies and models of investment behaviour show that the prospect of higher demand is the most important determinant of investment, taking it for granted that, on the whole, firms will not want to indulge in unprofitable investment. The level of interest rates is obviously an important determinant of profitability, though experience suggests that interest rates are difficult to predict.

But the problem that concerns us here – namely the prospect of a Britain without oil or with less oil – is the very problem that was worrying most corporate forecasters who were drawing up their plans for the rest of the decade. The Government's mismanagement of the oil windfall had essentially been at the macro-economic level. The prospect of lower oil revenues made industry depressed and concerned for the future. But it is one of the arguments of this book that, in an important sense, the worries about oil revenues have become a surrogate for the real concern: the Government's failure to pursue a sufficiently expansionary macro-economic policy at an appropriate exchange rate – both of which should have boosted the confidence of businessmen.

Industry was not helped to form an optimistic assessment of the future by consideration of the evidence of the recent past. The justification for the Government's financial strategy was, we had all been told, that it would provide a stable framework for business and industry and would eliminate the vicissitudes and uncertainties of the past. But apart from providing an atmosphere in which it was clear that the Government would do almost anything to avoid an acceleration in inflation and almost anything to lower public-sector borrowing, the Government's medium-term financial strategy had little else to offer businessmen. During the discredited 'Keynesian' days of the 1950s, 1960s and early 1970s, industry knew that Governments were committed, whenever the inflation and balance of payments constraints made this possible, to an expansionary economic environment.

In the 1980s, however, this has not been the case, and the Government has tried to make a virtue of its not being the case. The Government has refused to intervene. It has tried to keep inflation and government spending down and has left the rest to business. One obvious side-effect of this stance has been that business could not expect the traditional counter-cyclical boost from government spending. Business might, as President Reagan's boom in the USA reminded us, do exceedingly well out of government contracts – if the contracts were there. But the Thatcher Government has not believed in stimulating the economy this way.

If there was no commitment to macro-economic stimulus when the balance of payments allowed this, because of the North Sea's contribution, what on earth would be the Government's approach if the expected balance of payments crisis occurred? And why was the Government washing its hands of the possibility of economic reconstruction in advance? Was Britain going to have to wait in gloomy anticipation for a crash in the pound some time in the second half of the decade, as the NEDO analysis implied? Or was the foreign-exchange market, which can in theory anticipate these things, going to react earlier?

There was a warning shot early in 1985, when the pound came under severe pressure in the foreign-exchange markets and the Government reacted by briefly reintroducing its own interest-rate guideline, MLR, at 12 per cent and then encouraging the clearing banks to raise their base lending rates to 14 per cent.

The fall in the pound coincided with a worldwide strengthening of the dollar, and the British Government did its best to represent the pound's fall as no more than the obverse of the dollar's rise, a rise that was affecting many other currencies. But in January 1985 the pound fell sharply not only against the dollar but also against the West German mark, and it was signs of a 'free fall' against the latter that led the Government to give the signal for a panic rise in interest rates.

Although the pound had fallen considerably against the dollar in 1984, it still ended the year at an average level, against all the major currencies, that was no lower than that of 1976. Meanwhile costs had risen far faster than in most competitor countries, so that the 'real' exchange rate was much higher.[15] In January 1985 it fell to new lows amid much talk in the foreign-exchange markets about the UK's being a 'one-commodity' (oil) country.

It was difficult to take such talk seriously. The very week in which the Government was forced to raise interest rates was the week when Norway – much more dependent on oil than the UK – actually lowered them in order to discourage funds from flowing into that country. This suggested it was not so much worry about a falling oil price that was concerning the foreign-exchange markets as a more fundamental reappraisal of the UK's economic performance – the first sign perhaps of anticipation, on the part of the markets, of the problems of a Britain without oil. The pound recovered sharply in the first half of 1985 by 25 per cent against the dollar and by 15 per cent against the other major currencies. This was at the price of continuously high interest rates, so that by June the CBI was complaining to the Government about both high interest rates and the effect the strong pound was once more having on the UK's international competitiveness.

5 False Dawns, False Explanations

We can now begin, I hope, to draw some of the threads together and to see how the long-term relative decline of the UK fits in with the more recent recession and how they both interact with the use of the North Sea oil. The $64,000 question is: Where do we go from here? In this chapter I shall examine what I regard as the false dawns and false explanations that have been in plentiful supply during recent years. In the last chapters I shall attempt to offer a constructive alternative.

Explanations of the longer-term British economic problem were legion well before the advent of North Sea oil and certainly did not cease with its arrival. As we have seen, it was widely hoped that, sensibly used, North Sea oil might contribute towards the solution of the longer-term problem. Not only do we not find that borne out in practice; we actually discover that the longer-term problem was exacerbated during the period when the oil revenues were rising to their peak.

Meanwhile there have been plenty of rationalizations of the recent recession and of the economic misfortunes that have co-incided with the exploitation of the North Sea. These were ac-companied by assertions from the Government first that recovery was just around the corner and, later, that it was well under way.

There is an extensive body of economic, political and sociological work on the reasons for the relative decline of the British economy, and it is not the prime purpose of this book to rake over that ground again. After many years of exposure to those reading lists, I am not sure even now that I have ever read a satisfactory explanation.

Many works provide an exhaustive survey of all the possible

factors that could be held responsible for Britain's relative decline and leave the reader to judge for himself. Others, whether or not they do this first, tend to pin the principal responsibility on a narrow range of causes, often on only one. The latter constitute what Professor Sir Jim Ball, late of the London Business School, characterizes as the OBE (One Big Explanation) school.

Understanding has not always been helped by the exaggeration with which so many participants in the debate are tempted to present their case in order to attract attention. For example, to read or listen to some critics, you would hardly believe that, in spite of all the horrors, the UK had managed to double its standard of living in the twenty-five years after the Second World War. At the other extreme there is the case of the touching 'farewell to Britain' book written by the *Washington Post*'s former London correspondent, who firmly believed that Britain had got it right and that what he regarded as the emphasis on leisure rather than work here was a perfectly sensible way of going about things.[1] The problem that this author seemed to ignore was that we needed to do the work to pay for quite a lot of the leisure we liked. As the analysis already presented in this book shows, the particular form our leisure preferences take is having deleterious effects on the trade balance that may well prove unsustainable.

It seems to me to be easier to find explanations for cyclical problems than for the secular ones in the British economy. One can, as we have seen, point to clear indications in the way in which economic policy was handled between 1979 and 1985 to explain the sharp rise in unemployment during those years. One can also list all kinds of factors that may have had something to do with Britain's relatively poor economic performance over the years. There is the fact that we were first with the Industrial Revolution; there is the alleged bias against industry on the part of society generally and in the educational system; there is the union problem; there is the question of the quality of British management; there is the End of Empire argument – that we relied on captive markets for years; there are mistakes and discontinuity in successive Governments' economic policies; there is the political system itself ...

We all have our favourite explanation, with the union problem probably taking the lion's share of the blame. I have myself always been as suspicious of the union explanation as one is when told by one party to a divorce that the blame lies entirely on the other side. Looking at the industry closest, as it were, to my own home, I do not think it would be wise to lay the blame for poor performance in Fleet Street entirely at the unions' door: the behaviour of managements over the years has not exactly helped the union problem.

What is abundantly clear is that the general mix of British managements, unions and governmental intervention has produced what economists would call 'less than optimal' results. It is also fairly evident that Britain, in spite of all its faults, managed to be carried along on the back of the post-war boom. It would seem to follow that it must be in Britain's interest to encourage economic policies that foster booming world conditions rather than, as happened in 1979–84, to do its best, in international forums, to promote the reverse.

The easiest thing to identify in British economic performance is a conservatism, a resistance to change, that has been with us for many years. This is the common factor behind many of the explanations and symptoms of poor performance, as we saw in Chapter 4. It would seem, however, that one is likely to encounter less resistance to change in an expansionary economic environment than in a restrictive or repressive one. It was clear that during the 1984–5 miners' strike opposition to Arthur Scargill was accompanied, on the part of large sections of the general public, by sympathy for the plight of the miners themselves – namely, the lack of alternative opportunities for them and, in particular, for the future of their communities.

A key question about the Thatcher administration is whether it did something to soften the country's resistance to change or actually managed to harden attitudes. My own suspicion is very much the latter. And by in the end ducking out of the debate about how best to utilize the North Sea windfall, the Government surely neglected a major opportunity to improve the climate for investment in new industries and, indeed, to assist the changes it so strongly felt were needed.

Adrian Hamilton has made an interesting point by looking at the situation another way and by asking whether one could seriously believe that the French or the Germans would have handled the North Sea in the way the British did.[2] Economists can give answers about what is likely to happen if the factors of production are used, or mixed, in a particular way and about what is likely to be the consequence of various government actions and the response of people in their jargon guise as 'consumers' or 'investors'. They are in the business not of changing people's behaviour, merely of observing it and drawing what conclusions they can.

In the end the Thatcher experiment seemed to be a rather naive experiment in social engineering, through which it was hoped that the behaviour and attitudes of the unions would somehow change and that this would make life easier for entrepreneurs. Life was eased for entrepreneurs in all sorts of ways with tax cuts for the higher-income brackets, but the promotion of expanding markets, which are the first requirement of successful business, was hardly encouraged by the economic policy, as the abysmal figure of 1 per cent growth in five years for the non-oil economy demonstrates.

We can reasonably narrow the search down to two fundamental objectives and, before going on to offer a possible solution, should briefly examine a number of the palliatives that are certainly not solutions but have frequently been offered by the Government – and sometimes by well-meaning observers. Even if identifying the truest causes of Britain's secular economic problem is not easy, it is a start if one identifies those routes that would merely take us backwards.

The objectives are higher living standards and reasonably full employment. Perhaps the first threat to those objectives identified by the Thatcher administration was the world recession. But it is abundantly clear from comparative OECD statistics that the recession in the UK after 1979 was much deeper than that suffered in most industrial countries.[3]

We were told, for a while, that the black economy would somehow fill the gap caused by deficiencies in the wider picture. It always seemed strange that leaders who prided themselves on Victorian values, and adopted a high moral tone in formulating their economic strictures and beliefs, should attempt to take refuge in the shadier areas of tax avoidance and law-breaking as compensation for what they could not achieve on a wider front. But they also made fundamental mistakes in somehow managing to convince themselves that the black economy was a substitute for the white economy, when in fact the two were closely related. It was never likely that there would be a sudden upsurge in domestic plumbing and house repairs that would offset the devastating effects of the huge cuts in public-sector expenditure on housing. In fact, there was a recession in the black economy too – as one would only have expected.

Services? We were comfortingly reassured that in this sphere there would be a great growth in employment that would offset the damage being wrought to employment in the manufacturing sector. Here again, the service economy was badly affected by the recession. And although the OECD figures I have quoted confirm the general view that services have done better than manufacturing in recent years, the difference has not been sufficient to make up for lack of employment opportunities elsewhere. Moreover, much of the growth in services employment in the 1970s came in the public sector, which the Government has deliberately cut back.

Small businesses? The Thatcher Government contained Ministers from the top downwards who could hardly pronounce the phrase 'small businesses' without adopting the reverential tones more suitable for the inside of a cathedral. I once heard the Environment Secretary, Patrick Jenkin, wax eloquently to an audience in the Mansion House about his dream that up and down the country people would start opening small businesses in their garages and that thereby a great economic revolution would take place. I thought at first that he was joking.

Similarly, both the Prime Minister and her second Chancellor, Nigel Lawson, seemed to become obsessed with statistics showing that much of the growth in employment in the US in the past ten years had been provided by small business. At no stage did they appear to make the connection that small businesses live in the same economic environment as large businesses; that the two sectors need each other; and that the employment generated by the small businesses was in many cases an indirect effect of demand from the larger firms that had been generated by expansionary economic policies.

The Chancellor, in particular, gave the impression in his Mais lecture in 1984 that, in contrast to the UK, the picture in the USA over the previous decade had been one of the steady growth of jobs – many of them in the small-business sector – thanks to the 'enterprise culture' that prevailed over there, which Ministers would like to introduce into Britain. (This was after British Ministers had already had a good five years in which to do this.) Another interesting point about the US economy was that unemployment had, in fact, risen from 7 per cent to over 11 per cent between 1979 and 1982 and had fallen back towards 7 per cent again after a wholesale reversal of economic policy and as a result of an old-style Keynesian fiscal expansion. There was nothing 'steady' about the course of the US economy over those years. And while the US may well have an 'enterprise culture' and be more dynamic at creating jobs, it had such a culture during all those years when unemployment in the UK was much lower – not to mention the period 1979–82, when unemployment soared under tight economic policies. Lord Kaldor has suggested: 'The huge rise in employment in the United States – for 19 million, or 25 per cent of the total amount of employment in ten years is indeed a very big figure – was the consequence of large doses of reflationary stimuli introduced by two Republican Presidents [Ford and Reagan].'[4]

A number of rationalizations have been popular in recent years to explain away Britain's unemployment crisis. They have been convenient for the Government, although not always stemming from Ministers at first. Indeed, some have even been propagated by well-meaning opponents of the Government's economic policies.

First, there has been a revival of the scare that technological progress was putting people out of work and that, for this reason alone, full unemployment is a thing of the past. This is an explanation that has been regularly trotted out for over a hundred years. As Douglas Jay pointed out in a recent book, 'Technical progress was not suddenly discovered in June 1979.'[5]

This explanation is very reminiscent of the 'automation' scare of the 1950s. It puts all the emphasis on the people displaced when new methods of production are implemented – capital-deepening – and ignores the historically important employment-creation effects of capital-widening as new discoveries are made and new products brought into use for the first time. Moreover, the statistics for productivity growth suggest that, if anything, technological progress has been slower, at least in its application, since the 1970s than in the 1950s and 1960s.[6]

Technological progress is good not only in bringing a higher standard of living to many – as Schumpeter pointed out, the silk stockings for whose production Marie-Antoinette employed thousands of people are now available to all[7] – but it also eases the harshness of man's lot, so that, for example, mechanical diggers can do the work of the chain gangs of the past. The experience of the 1950s and 1960s showed that technological progress could be accompanied by periods of rapid economic growth and impressively full employment. A look around the world – let alone a look around our own country – suggests that there is enough deprivation and unsatisfied need to take full advantage of technical progress, and all the available manpower, if only we can order things better. Which brings us to a related fallacy: the idea that the only answer is to meet the present employment crisis in Britain by resorting to work-sharing and early retirement.

For one thing, these ideas seem to assume that there is a fixed 'lump' of work and to ignore all the unsatisfied needs of the world. If we had somehow achieved an earthly paradise, in which all the conceivable wants of the population were being satisfied, then it might make sense to embark on policies of early retirement and work-sharing. But it is evident that we are a long way from such a complacent state.

One must distinguish, also, between the longer-term trend towards a shorter working week – brought about by, in effect, the desires of the workforce – and promoting a shorter working week simply because it is believed that there will never again be enough work to go round. If a man's preference is for a shorter week and the money he gains from the hours he chooses to work is sufficient, then that is fair enough. But if a shorter working week is forced upon him, and for less pay, then that is a very different matter. He will not be so pleased. Now, if the sacrifice is necessary, then that is one thing. But, as I hope to show in the next chapter, it is not necessary; there are better ways of conducting economic policy, and they are available to us. There is no need to assume that all the work opportunities are exhausted and that therefore work has to be shared out through shorter weeks and earlier retirement. Here again, this is perfectly consistent with the possibility that some people, who have the wish and the savings, may choose, of their own free will, to retire early.

We come finally to the most bizarre excuse of all: this is the argument that gained quite remarkably wide currency during the first Thatcher administration and was still widely quoted during the early phases of the second. It is the argument that was expressed sometimes by the question 'What is the alternative?' and sometimes by the straight assertion, 'There is no alternative' (or Tina, as it became known for short in Westminster and Whitehall). This argument was never logically defensible. But the argument was probably shorthand for the view that the alternative was unthinkable, that we could not go back to the bad old ways – rip-roaring inflation, the unions running the country and so on.

Now there was, and probably still is, a lot of sympathy for this view, but there is a wide gap between tolerance of economic policies that allow unemployment to rise inexorably and resort to policies that revive the spectre of some of the worst moments of the 1970s. It is somewhere in this middle ground that we must look to find a way out of the present economic mess and the chance to prepare Britain for the days when it will begin the transition towards a Britain without oil. That will be the subject of Chapter 6.

6 Re-employing Britain

RE-EMPLOYING BRITAIN

The economic crisis now facing Britain bears some resemblance to the problems facing British Governments after the First and the Second World War. War and mobilization brought full employment; after the First World War successive Governments failed to manage a successful transition to a fully employed peacetime economy. Britain was never a 'land fit for heroes'. After the Second World War things were very different: the lessons of the inter-war period had been learned. There was a national and, even more important, an international commitment to policies of expansion and full employment. The transition was successful and was followed by some twenty-five years of unparalleled prosperity.

After the First World War there was plenty of evidence that the British economy was in secular or relative decline. The debate about Britain's loss of industrial muscle and markets had begun in the 1860s, akin to the deindustrialization debate in the 1970s that we discussed earlier in this book. The economic history books are replete with examples of how Britain lost out to Germany and the USA, of how it was too dependent on the 'old' or 'basic' industries such as coal and steel.

In the 1920s and 1930s the worries about this secular decline were exacerbated by the failure to pursue appropriate economic policies. Going back to the gold standard in 1925 was the equivalent, because of the high exchange rate at which the pound was pegged to the dollar, of the policies that permitted the overvaluation of the pound in 1979 to 1981 and severely hampered British industry's ability to compete against other countries. The deflationary policies of the 1920s and 1930s have also been echoed in the policies adopted by the Thatcher Government since 1979.

For a long period after the Second World War successive 'Butskellite' British Governments pursued expansionary economic policies. At times they attempted to defend unsustainable exchange rates, but on the whole, until the late 1970s, they did not indulge in the positive perversion of encouraging a self-destructive *rise* in the exchange rate.

We are now faced with the task not of transforming a large element of the workforce from wartime to peacetime employment but of providing work for a large army of peacetime unemployed. How is this going to be achieved?

The key to the full employment of the economy lies now, as manifestly it has lain since Keynes's contribution, with sufficient effective demand in the economy – or, to put it another way, with sufficient final expenditure on all goods and services, public and private, current and capital. If resources are left unemployed, as they have been prodigally in terms of both labour and capital in recent years, then it is manifest that there is a deficiency of effective demand.

Recent experience has been a classic demonstration of what Keynesians have always known: that, left to itself, the economy will not necessarily so order itself that a return to full employment is inevitable – *a fortiori*, if the policies of the Government are designed to keep the lid on the economy. The obsession with keeping the PSBR down in recent years is just such a design. Estimates vary, of course, but if non-oil output had been allowed to grow at anything like the rate of the previous five or ten years since 1979, the British country's effective demand, and output, would have been between £30 billion and £40 billion higher by now. This completely dwarfs, among other things, the £12.5 billion or so of

97

revenue to the Exchequer from the North Sea. (Given that loss of output, it is nevertheless fair to ask the question: Where on earth would we have been without North Sea oil?)

There may be deindustrialization worries – and they have been expressed in plenty in this book. But all experience also shows that if the lid is kept on the economy and expansion is not encouraged, then there is little incentive for industry to make the adaptive leap into new products, new processes, new industries. It may do this to some extent, but this will not be sufficient, as we have seen all too clearly, to bring about full employment.

The situation we are faced with in 1985, however, is that a golden opportunity for Britain to expand without a balance of payments constraint has been wasted. It is, one might say, so much oil under the bridge. Once again, unlike the proverbial Irishman, we have to start from here whether we like it or not.

The two questions addressed by Keynesians and monetarists alike are: What effect will expansion have on the inflation rate? And how long can it be sustained without a balance of payments crisis? By expansion I am not talking about the climb back to the top of the trough, and a little above it, that we have experienced in the past two years. I am talking about an expansion that will bring unemployment down and employ the British workforce more effectively by satisfying Britain's own economic needs and making a decent contribution to those of the underdeveloped world.

(Talking of the underdeveloped world, we do need to maintain a sense of proportion. Some of these countries are in effect trying to make leaps that took the advanced industrial countries several centuries. They cannot, as it were, be expected to achieve this overnight; nor, I suspect, do the precepts of history, evolution and sensible social adjustment demand it. But there is a considerable difference between falling short of idealists' aspirations for a better and more prosperous Third World and suffering many countries, notably in Africa, to go backwards when we have the knowledge and techniques to help them much more.)

The effect of expansionary policies on the inflation rate depends crucially on two things, one of which is considerably more important than the other. The lesser one is 'externally induced' cost increases, notably in prices of raw materials such as oil. The greater is wages and salary costs, which account for over two-thirds of total costs. The depression of raw-material prices generally in recent years shows how far not only Britain but the entire world economy is from a high level of effective demand pressing on resources. There seems to be little to fear from that quarter; and even if such a fear develops, the lesson of recent economic history is that the key thing is to try to stop union wage-bargainers from being allowed to index themselves to external cost increases beyond domestic governmental control. That was what prompted the wages explosion of 1974–5, and we are still living with the consequences: it has contributed in no small measure to the extreme reaction that we can never expand again. We can, but we must learn the lessons of the past.

The only answer to the danger of the wage-inflation spiral is to be aware of it, to educate people and to try to guard against it. Since even well-educated members of the Thatcher Cabinet such as John Biffen, then Chief Secretary to the Treasury, were declaring in speeches made in 1979–80 that wages do not cause inflation, I assume that there is considerable potential for the education of less fortunate members of society in this matter.

The idea of cuts in real wages is a wonderfully ironic replay of the ideas that circulated in the 1920s and 1930s, when deflation and a high exchange rate produced an analagous situation. A fall in wages, aimed at a fall in real wages, may simply cause a fall in prices and leave no change in the real wage. But, other things being given, a fall in the real wage lowers effective demand even further, thereby compounding the unemployment problem. The key, as always, is what happens to effective demand. A fall in real wages when a country devalues its currency at full employment levels is a quite different affair; it is necessary in order to divert resources to exports. On the other hand, it is important, from the point of view of international competitiveness, that a rise in the price level as a result of a fall in the pound does not lead to a wage-inflation scramble that removes the competitiveness gain. If this restraint involves a temporary fall in the relative real wage, it is a case of *reculer pour mieux sauter*.

But I think the most succinct comment I have yet seen on the real wage-cutting school – which, for some reason, is largely synonymous with those who believe incomes policies have been tried and have failed – is that by Douglas Jay: 'Whatever else is true, it cannot be true that a policy of making actual pay cuts is more practicable than one of restraining increases.'[1] (It is also worth bearing in mind one of the points made in the NEDO study cited earlier: that high real wages tend to be associated with the better and more advanced sectors of British industry and low real wages with the backward sectors.)

There are four known routes to low wage inflation. One is to abolish wages and to reintroduce slavery, which I take it we can rule out.

A second is to keep the lid on the economy via high and rising unemployment, so that wages are kept down through fear. That has been, in practice, the method of the Thatcher Government. It is morally reprehensible, economically wasteful and potentially seditious. Furthermore, the same objection can be made to it that the Thatcherites made about the Keynesian economic stimuli in the past: namely, that it is like a drug that has less and less effect as people become accustomed to it. Even now, with 3.5 million people unemployed, the rate of wage inflation is remarkably high. The next logical step is to move to 5 million or 10 million unemployed in order to keep wages under control. That would provoke even the placid British to revolution.

The third route is magically to disarm militant wage-bargainers and to reduce confrontation generally in British industry by instituting some variety of the co-operative, profit-sharing, partnership or workers'-control schemes that have been in the textbooks and pamphlets for several hundreds of years but have been introduced only in relative isolation so far. This route would lead, its proponents hope, to the burial of the 'them and us' attitudes that are thought to bedevil British industrial relations and to lie at the heart of our inflationary problems.

I have nothing against these ideas. They sound absolutely splendid. And, as I have already pointed out, they have been around for several hundreds of years. I also think that it may well be that their time has come and that we may be about to experience an acceleration in the journey towards them.

One thing is absolutely certain, however: they are unlikely to be introduced overnight or to become soon so prevalent that confrontation in Britain will become a thing of the past and sweet, co-operative reason will be all the rage. They do not solve the problem of how we should reverse the unemployment trend in the next year or so. And by reverse I do not merely mean bring about a slight fall: I mean seriously reduce unemployment to nearer 1 million than 2 million, to a level at which unemployment and vacancies balance, allowing for job search.

We are led inexorably to the fourth route towards lower cost-push and wage inflation – namely, incomes policies in some form. The standard objection to incomes policies, as I have remarked, is that they have been tried and have failed. This objection does not stand up to serious scrutiny. The truth about incomes policies is that they have been tried sporadically, have worked for a time and have then broken down. Not the least of the factors behind their breakdown is the behaviour of the two major political parties in the 1970s: both the Conservatives and the Labour Party were at various times 100 per cent in favour of incomes policies and 100 per cent against. The promise of free collective bargaining or a policy that assumed that wages do not cause inflation was obviously a very tempting one for trade unions, which had previously seen themselves as knuckling under. There is, in fact, no alternative to some form of incomes policy unless we are content to rely indefinitely on high unemployment as the principal anti-inflationary weapon.

The problem with our experience of incomes policies so far in this country is that we have not tried hard enough. There has not been the cross-party consensus on the need for sensible behaviour over wages, in return for government commitment to expansionary policies, that is taken almost for granted in Japan, the Scandinavian countries and Austria. In West Germany the commitment to low inflation and an unofficial, unbureaucratic incomes policy has been evident for years. But what West Germany itself has not come to terms with is its own importance in the European and the world economy. In spite of its low inflation rate – forecast at 2 per cent for 1985 – West Germany has been reluctant to take major expansionary measures.

This brings us conveniently to the other constraint on the expansionary policies in the UK: the balance of payments. West Germany does not have a serious balance of payments problem, in spite of the fact that it is an importer of oil. Quite the contrary. Nor has it a serious inflation problem. The country has tended to do well out of the rapid growth of world trade associated with the expansionary policies pursued for many years after the Second World War. More recently it has faced high unemployment in spite of its success with what are known as the 'economic fundamentals'. Although it is the most important West European economy, West Germany has not seen itself as having Europe-wide (let alone worldwide) responsibilities for economic leadership. In recent years, as it is such an important exporter, its performance has reflected the wider European recession, but the Government has done little to offset this via a deliberate attempt at domestic expansion. West Germany wants the growth to come from somewhere else and then to participate in it. Its leaders also subscribe, to a large extent, to the self-generating, neo-classical school of economic policy that, as we have seen in the case of the UK, can produce a mild revival in the economy but not sufficient to make serious inroads into the unemployment problem.

France, by contrast, tried in the early phases of the Mitterrand presidency to expand its economy in a classic Keynesian way but ran into balance of payments problems because it got out of step with the UK and West Germany, where more deflationary policies were being pursued. Its expansion led to higher imports and a balance of payments and exchange-rate crisis. The reaction of the French Government was to abandon its brave attempt to expand; instead it retrenched. France wanted to hold its head up high in international forums. Policy became geared to protecting the franc. (France had not helped its case with the foreign-exchange market judges by allowing large wage increases, nationalizing the banks and simultaneously being rather cavalier in trying to get interest rates down.)

The French problem, the German problem and the British problem are all part of the same conundrum, and the OECD has published some excellent work analysing this. Any one European country trying to expand alone risks a balance of payments crisis that need not occur at all if all were to expand together. A co-ordinated expansion would mean that, like boats in the same harbour, they could all rise with the tide; there would be enough water for them all. Such are the links between countries' economies that a gentle, simultaneous expansion can have marked cumulative effects; the proposal is certainly not for an inflationary surge.[2]

Taken as a broad group, the European economy is about the size of that of the USA if one only counts the EEC countries and even larger if one includes the non-EEC countries. Europe should not be, and does not need to be, entirely dependent on the USA and its budgetary/interest-rate policies: it has the ability, the techniques and the muscle to expand its way out of recession. And whereas individual European countries have a large foreign-trade sector – amounting to between 25 per cent and 30 per cent of GDP, the European economy as a whole has a foreign-trade sector of proportions similar to those of the USA.

The reason for this is simply that much of the 'foreign' trade of individual West European countries is trade with one another. If they all decided to expand together, the effect would be the equivalent of the enormous growth that occurred in the USA under the expansionary policies of 1983–4. The resulting trade expansion would not be 'foreign' in the sense that much of it would be within Europe. There is no need for any of the European countries to run into a serious balance of payments problem if they have a joint economic expansion of sensible proportions.

Although I say there is no need for individual European countries to face serious balance of payments problems during a co-ordinated expansion, this statement begs two further questions: Does the mechanism for a co-ordinated European expansion exist? And would the good old UK, in spite of the theoretical attractions of this, have a special problem of its own?

The answer to the first question is that, through the regular meetings of the Council of Ministers and through the Brussels bureaucracy that serves them, European leaders would have little difficulty, if they put their minds to it, in co-ordinating an expansionary economic policy that brought unemployment down in all their countries. What they need to do, however, is to change the emphasis of European discussions from concentration on the relatively small, albeit important, agricultural and budget problem to concentration on the wider issues. This they have so far singularly (I should perhaps say collectively) failed to do.

The second query brings us back to one of the concerns that has emerged in the course of the book. Is the British economy now so debilitated that, even under a Europe-wide, co-ordinated expansion, it would not be able to cope? By this I mean: Would even a European expansion in which Britain played an active part produce balance of payments problems for the UK, in spite of the £20 billion-plus contribution to the balance of payments from the North Sea? (The huge current-account balance of payments surpluses of the early 1980s were already down to modest figures by 1984–5, despite the oil contribution.)

There are many who think this, which is why in the debates about the shape of the 1985 Budget much emphasis was placed by the more expansionist-minded critics on public-sector investment in the infrastructure of the economy – roads, sewers, housing and the environment generally – on the grounds that not only were these desirable candidates in themselves for new investment but also that they would have a low import content and would therefore not threaten the balance of payments as much as would an expansionary boost from lower taxation.

However, these arguments were being advanced in the context of a distinct absence of co-ordinated European expansion. A major expansion in the March 1985 Budget – which, needless to say, was not even contemplated – would have taken risks with the balance of payments.

How the British economy would fare in a co-ordinated expansion remains to be seen. One thing is certain: it could not do worse than under an unco-ordinated expansion. A second, simple, point is that one has to start, or start again, somewhere. British industry may be in a debilitated condition, but then so it was after the First and the Second World War. The continual obsession with lowering the PSBR figures as the central aim of economic policy is hardly going to do the trick. If the economy runs into problems during an attempt at real, sustained expansion, then options for dealing with them will have to be considered. But the failure to make that attempt is likely to make the underlying problems even worse.

One further point: it should be emphasized that in spite of the losses to industrial capacity suffered in recent years and the capital shortages pinpointed by the OECD study cited earlier, there remains a considerable body of resources – especially of labour but also of capital – that is heavily under-utilized.[3] It is possible to exaggerate the risks to inflation when there is so much spare capacity. It is difficult to envisage how the longer-term capital shortage can be met if the economy is not stimulated in the short term. And the fact that we have failed to do so already does not mean we should go on postponing the reconstruction of the capital stock that is needed in the medium term to restore employment and in the longer term to cope with the problems of a Britain without oil.

7 A Change of Policy

It is tempting to ask how Britain would have weathered the six years 1979–85 without the windfall benefits of North Sea oil, but that is to beg a question: Would economic policy have been conducted in quite this fashion without the oil?

In a sense it was rising North Sea oil revenues that made the Thatcher economic experiment possible. Important aspects of that experiment were the desire to 'bash the unions' and the philosophical (or religious) belief that it was the job of business left to itself, not of government economic policy, to promote employment. (Improvements at the micro level would help employment, said the Chancellor, Nigel Lawson, in his 1984 Mais lecture. Macroeconomic policy would concentrate on the defeat of inflation.)

A macro-economic policy that did not aim to promote employment did not aim at the stimulation of demand and output either. What was happening to manufacturing industry – and illustrated graphically in the non-oil trade deficit – was more than offset in the accounts by the huge oil surplus. The Government was not forced to pay serious attention to what was happening to manufacturing industry because there was no balance of payments crisis. This meant that the Government's exchange-rate policy was not geared to the longer-term (or even the medium-term) needs of the UK's international competitiveness. And the rapidly rising contribution of oil to the Budget accounts enabled the Government to appear to be sticking to its policy of containing public-sector borrowing. There was no need for a U-turn.

Without the oil revenues, it is difficult to see how the Government would ever have got anywhere near its borrowing targets. This would almost certainly have forced it to rethink its policy of making cuts in public-sector borrowing such a central strand of the strategy; it might even have led to the conclusion that one way of raising government revenues is to run the economy at a higher level of demand, output and employment.

North Sea activities created, directly and indirectly, some 80,000 jobs in Scotland, while unemployment in the rest of the economy rose by over 2 million between 1979 and 1985. Sir Ian Gilmour wrote: 'Sometimes it seems that a "real" job is one that has not yet been destroyed by the Treasury.'[1] Sir Douglas Wass, Permanent Secretary at the Treasury from 1974 to 1984, has suggested that the stance of macro-economic policy explains not only the sharp falls in manufacturing output and employment of the past six years but also the secular trend identified in the NEDO and deindustrialization papers discussed earlier. 'A plausible explanation of the fall in manufacturing output in the past fifteen years is that for much of that period we have operated restrictive fiscal and monetary policies and have been running the economy below its potential – or at least below the potential it had before the period of restriction began.' Over much of that period, Sir Douglas said, the exchange rate was 'too high'.[2]

Britain faces a huge unemployment problem. The official government figure is over 3 million. If one allows for those categories that have simply been removed from the register in various ways, or for people who are on assorted artificial 'work-creation' schemes, the true unemployment total is over 4 million.

The economy had its troubles before 1979, and we have seen that there were worries that deindustrialization had set in during the 1970s. By this was meant the fact that Britain could not cope with rapid expansion without moving into a balance of payments crisis. The attempt to avoid such a crisis had been the theme of much of the economic debate of the previous two decades.

Nevertheless, until recent years the British economy had somehow managed. Unemployment was 'only' 1.3 million in June 1979, when the Thatcher administration took office, promising to reduce it ('Labour isn't working') from this level and to cure the longer-term problems of the economy as well. Although Britain had performed relatively badly in previous years, it had still taken its share of the fruits of the post-war boom.

The advent of North Sea oil, at a time of general energy shortage, gave the country an unprecedented opportunity to do something about its chronic balance of payments problem. It was offered the chance of expanding without running into balance of payments constraints and thus of using some of the proceeds of the North Sea both for investment in the energy sources that would surely be needed in the future and for rebuilding what was widely regarded as its debilitated manufacturing base.

The build-up of the North Sea began under the Wilson/Callaghan Governments of 1974–9 but experienced its real dynamic effect in 1979–85, when oil production doubled to about 120 million tonnes and government revenues soared from £0.5 billion to £12 billion a year. By 1985 oil was contributing more than £20 billion to the balance of payments (a sixfold increase over the period).[3]

But much of this period coincided with the worst recession since the Second World War, and the contribution from the North Sea almost got lost in the overall figures. The most disturbing link was that between the rise in the contribution of oil to the balance of payments and the fall in the contribution of manufacturing industry. By 1983 the UK was a net importer of manufactured goods.

The idea that somehow the acceleration of Britain's manufacturing decline in the first half of the 1980s was directly 'caused' by North Sea oil does not stand up to close examination, as we have seen. The problems of the 1980s were caused by a combination of strict monetary and fiscal policies manifested, among other ways, in too high an exchange rate. Despite the belief held by the

Government for a time, the evidence is that possession of North Sea oil itself exerted only a minor influence on the exchange rate. These things are always, to a certain extent, a matter of judgement, but reputable evidence suggests that it was not the North Sea itself but the way in which it – and economic policy generally – was handled that caused problems with the exchange rate and with international competitiveness.

The idea that the decline of manufacturing was somehow inevitable does not bear much scrutiny either. It is clear from comparative OECD statistics that, in many economies that are already at a more advanced stage of industrialization than is the UK, manufacturing output has continued to grow. There is no OECD-wide trend away from manufacturing. Nor is competition from the newly industrializing countries causing a decline in manufacturing elsewhere. Again, the stance of economic policy seems much the most sensible explanation in the case of the UK.

The problem facing the UK in 1985 is that the contribution of the North Sea to the balance of payments has reached its peak. The only question, even after allowing for the most optimistic assumptions about future oil production and discoveries, is at what rate it will fall, during the second half of the 1980s and the 1990s, on the long road towards what we might call non-self-sufficiency.

The UK had huge balance of payments surpluses during the early part of the 1980s, the result of the build-up of the North Sea flows and of running the economy at well below its productive potential. This was just at the time when the earlier debate had indicated that it would be an appropriate moment not to worry about the effect of high demand on the balance of payments, precisely because of the contribution from the North Sea. In the mid-1980s the balance of payments surplus has almost been eroded. It may be argued that there is nothing wrong with such equilibrium, but expansion of demand will tend to move it towards deficit, and the pattern of the oil flows is certainly going to do so. There will thus, other things being given, be two adverse pressures on the balance of payments. In such circumstances it seems absurd, in the first half of 1985, for the Government to have made one of its main economic goals the defence of an unrealistic exchange rate.

Everything points to a fall in the exchange rate of the pound against non-dollar currencies as a necessary condition of making British manufacturing more competitive internationally again. It is very likely that market perceptions of the UK's medium-term problem played a part in the sterling crisis of January 1985, when the pound fell rapidly against all currencies, not just the dollar, although the principal explanation of that episode lay with incompetent briefing of the press about the Prime Minister's views on the exchange rate.

The January 1985 fall left the pound at a historically low level against the dollar, prompting the claim from both the Prime Minister and the Chancellor that it was under-valued. It became a prime objective of policy to steady the pound against the dollar and an implied objective for the pound to recover somewhat. The Bank of England's trade-weighted index of the pound's average value against the major currencies (1975 = 100) rose from a low of 70.6 in January 1985 to 81.3 at the end of June and nearly 85.0 in July. During the sterling crisis of 1976 the pound's index had fallen to 74.0; given the very different inflation performance of the UK *vis-à-vis* other countries since 1976, the real exchange rate was still uncomfortably high in July 1985 from the point of view of British industry's competitive position against non-dollar currencies.

The position in the summer of 1985, then, was that the UK was in any case faced, in the medium term, with a fall in the exchange rate to bring its foreign-trade position back into some sort of equilibrium. If this was likely to happen anyway, then the case for not being too concerned about the effects of expansionary policies on the balance of payments and the exchange rate seemed worth considering. Sir Alec Cairncross, for instance, a veteran of many Governments' problems with the exchange markets in his time, argued just this: that one should not deliberately seek a fall in the pound but equally should not be too worried if, as was likely, it happened as a result of expansionary policies.[4]

The lesson of six years of monetarism/Thatcherism/fiscal squeeze was merely to confirm what Keynesian economists had known from pre-war days: that 'neo-classical' assumptions about equilibrium in the economy were far removed from the real world and that some sort of equilibrium – albeit a deeply disruptive one – could be achieved at well below full employment levels. Indeed, the Chancellor, Nigel Lawson, seemed to be assuming that high unemployment was here to stay, under his policies, when he told an American journalist that 'economically and politically' Britain could get along adequately with 'double-digit' unemployment.[5]

Generally expansionary policies seem a necessary condition of reversing the recent decline in manufacturing and embarking on the road to full employment. As the 'Charter for Jobs' has pointed out,[6] things are so bad at present that the first move need not be called 'expansion', rather 'less deflation'. A further fall in the value of the pound against non-dollar currencies is also probably a necessary condition and likely in any case to result from more expansionary policies. Another necessary condition, as we have seen, is a serious cross-party commitment to the kind of unbureaucratic but sustainable incomes policy that is a standard feature of the German, Austrian, Scandinavian and Japanese scene.

Britain lived for many years after the war with fears about 'absolute decline' that never actually materialized. Even the participants in the deindustrialization debate of the 1970s were not sure whether they were not dealing with an 1870s problem. Some of the writing was certainly on the wall in the 1970s. What would have happened under a continuation of previous policies we do not know. But we do know what happened under policies that were justified by the strange and illogical slogan 'There is no alternative.'

Thus the movement to what *appears* to have been 'absolute decline' of manufacturing in the UK finally took place as a result not of a continuation of bad old ways but of seriously damaging economic policies. These produced a huge deficiency of demand in the economy. Deficiencies of demand can be reversed.

The policies that brought about the manufacturing decline were justified, on the part of their architects, as necessary to shake Britain up; what appears to have happened is that the country has been shaken, not stirred. The faster economic growth that we were promised in 1979, and the greater degree of investment, simply did not materialize. True, the inflationary situation in 1979–80 would probably have induced a pause, whatever the doctrines espoused by the Government. But its doctrines led to much worse inflation than it had inherited.

Since 1979 the UK has experienced a five-year period of the slowest economic growth since before the Second World War – in spite of the oil bonus. Nor does the prospect of a decline in the oil revenues appear to be producing an outburst of confidence among industrialists about the future climate for investment. For that they need a change in macro-economic policy and a commitment to economic expansion.

Postscript

I often tell people that, in spite of what may be regarded as the pessimistic nature of my writings on the economy, I am by nature an optimist (otherwise I should probably have emigrated long ago). One must distinguish between pessimism, which is a characteristic, and the attempt to be realistic and to tell the story as it is or as one thinks it is. During the first Thatcher administration, for instance, I was often accused of being negative and too pessimistic when writing my weekly column in the *Observer*. Many of those who made such accusations have since had second thoughts in the light of the Government's actual economic record.

It is always possible to look on the bright side. 'Why go on about the 13 per cent who are unemployed instead of the 87 per cent who are at work?' was a point that was often put to me. 'The standard of living of the vast majority of people in this country has never been higher' was another typical comment.

The obvious answer is that there is less need to worry about the 87 per cent, or those who are comfortably off. It is the imposition of needless suffering and needless hardship that shocks me; it is the belief – nay, knowledge – that we could order our affairs much better that motivates much of my writing.

During the last few years it has not, in any case, been a small percentage of the population that has been affected by unemployment or by cuts in the standards of the health and education services in the name of the PSBR. Unemployment among the young, at over 20 per cent, is much higher than the national average, and it has begun seriously to worry the middle classes. The threat to the welfare services and the nation's infrastructure has become apparent to all.

Then there is the unedifying spectacle of the British Government's cheese-paring when it comes to overseas aid when, in fact, we could easily afford to be more generous if we changed our economic policies. The public response to private appeals for African famine relief shows that, when they see the horrors of the world on their television screens, the British do care.

One theme of this book is that the wealth of the North Sea has so far been squandered and that the benefits it has brought have been dwarfed by the losses in output and revenue resulting from the self-inflicted wounds of economic policy. A further, 'pessimistic', theme is that all was not well with British industrial performance before the Thatcher Government managed to transform worries about relative decline in manufacturing industry into the achievement of actual decline.

The 'optimistic' note is that since the actual decline was the result of mistaken policies, it can be reversed. This does not rule out the need for this conservative country to order its economic affairs better if it wants to avoid relative decline. The message of the trend of the manufacturing trade balance is unmistakable; and while a sense of history suggests that something may turn up, the same sense of history is only too consistent with nothing turning up.

One of the points made in the deindustrialization conference referred to earlier was a warning:

Factors which explain a low relative *level* of productivity do not explain a widening productivity gap [*vis-à-vis* other industrial countries]. Here the question of cumulative causation comes in. It was pointed out that, within a country, it was not considered surprising that a region which had begun to decline should continue to do so; cumulative processes were clearly set up which tended to perpetuate the decline (unless strong policies were adopted). There could be much the same sort of decline for individual countries in a relatively free trading world. When it came to policy, however, a number of participants stressed the need for high and rising demand as a necessary (though not sufficient) condition for industrial success.[1]

The widening productivity gap was apparent in the 1970s, but the Thatcher Government subsequently claimed it had achieved a productivity 'miracle'. The latter claim was based on statistics for a very short period, and in fact the annual growth in manufacturing productivity between the second quarters of 1979 and 1984 was, at 2.5 per cent, greater than that recorded in the period 1973–8 but less than the 3.3 per cent per annum growth rate of 1953 to 1973.[2] This was hardly a miracle, but although comparative figures are not yet available, it looks as if, at least during the earlier period 1979 to 1982, the gap was no longer widening. But this was the period of the great 'shake-out' of labour and of a disturbing decline in manufacturing investment, the key to future productivity.[3]

Finally, I am indebted to what my Latin master used to refer to as 'one of those good German scholars' for the following 'optimistic' note. Britain may now be in deficit in its manufacturing trade for the first time since the Industrial Revolution, but Britain was first into the Industrial Revolution not just because it introduced machine production but also because it utilized a new source of energy – namely, coal. And the reason why Britain developed coal first was that it did not have the reserves of timber enjoyed by the well-forested continent of Europe.[4]

The economist Jevons thought in the nineteenth century that the British economy would cease to grow when the coal ran out. It is possible that the prospect of oil's running out may galvanize this country in the way that the prospect of timber's depletion did two hundred years ago, and it is comforting that, in spite of Jevons's fears, we have not yet run out of coal. But this is no excuse for the waste of resources of both oil and industrial output that we have suffered in the past five years. Let us hope that some lessons have been learned.

Notes

Introduction

1 See, for instance, Neil Hood and Stephen Young (eds.), *Industry, Policy and the Scottish Economy* (Edinburgh: Edinburgh University Press, 1984), and the work of Grant Baird and Alex Salmond, economists for the Royal Bank of Scotland.

1 Britain Before Oil

1 *Mrs Thatcher's Economic Experiment* (Harmondsworth: Penguin, 1984).
2 *ibid.*
3 Articles on the British economy written for Vickers da Costa, 1976–80, by W. Godley, Department of Applied Economics, University of Cambridge.
4 *Catalyst*, vol. 1, no. 1, 1985.
5 Stephen G. Hall and F. Atkinson, *Oil and the British Economy* (London: Croom Helm/New York: St Martin's, 1983).
6 Rt Hon. Nigel Lawson, Chancellor of the Exchequer, speech to the Cambridge Energy Conference, April 1984.
7 A. Hamilton, 'North Sea Impact', International Institute for Economic Research, 1978.
8 OECD, *Economic Outlook*, Paris, December 1983.
9 'Success in Invisibles' (report), Department of Trade and Industry, 1981.

2 The Impact of Oil

1 Gordon (now Lord) Richardson, Ashridge Lecture, 20 November 1980.

2 *Bank of England Quarterly Bulletin*, March 1982. (Much of the Bank's work on the impact of the North Sea was done by Christopher Allsopp, Fellow of New College, Oxford, then on secondment to the Bank.)

3 *ibid.*

4 Ashridge Lecture.

5 P. J. Forsyth and J. A. Kay, 'The Economic Implications of North Sea Oil Revenues', *Journal of the Institute of Fiscal Studies*, Vol. 1, No. 3, 1980.

6 Stephen G. Hall and F. Atkinson, *Oil and the British Economy* (London: Croom Helm/New York: St Martin's, 1983).

7 Evidence to House of Lords Select Committee on Overseas Trade, 11 December 1984.

8 NIESR, *Review*, November 1981.

9 Hall and Atkinson, *Oil and the British Economy*, p. 133.

10 OECD, *Economic Outlook*, Paris, December 1983.

11 'Monetarist Economics in Practice: the First Thatcher Government 1979–82', *Socialist Economic Review*, 1984.

12 'International Monetary Arrangements', Treasury and Civil Service Committee, March 1983.

13 OECD, *Historical Statistics 1960–1982*, Paris, 1984.

14 William Keegan, *Mrs Thatcher's Economic Experiment* (Harmondsworth: Penguin, 1984); J. Niehans, 'The Appreciation of Sterling – Causes, Effects, Policies', SSRC Money Study Group, 1981.

15 Hall and Atkinson, *Oil and the British Economy*.

16 'North Sea Oil and Structural Adjustment', Treasury Working Paper No. 22, 1982.

17 Wood, Mackenzie, North Sea Report, November 1984.

18 Oxford Economic Papers No. 33.

19 Hall and Atkinson, *Oil and the British Economy*.

20 Keegan, *Mrs Thatcher's Economic Experiment*.

21 Statements by J. Harvey-Jones, Chairman of ICI, Lord Kearton and others to House of Lords Select Committee on Overseas Trade, 24 April 1985.

3 Oil in Context

1 Frank Blackaby (ed.), *Deindustrialization* (London: NIESR, Heinemann, 1979).
2 Terry Barker and Vladimir Brailovsky (eds.), *Oil or Industry?: Energy, Industrialization and Economic Policy in Canada, Mexico, the Netherlands, Norway and the United Kingdom* (London/New York: Academic Press, 1981).
3 *ibid.*

4 Britain's Fundamental Economic Problem

1 W. Buiter and M. Miller, *The Macroeconomic Consequences of a Change in Regime: The UK under Mrs Thatcher*, Discussion Paper No. 179 (London: LSE, Centre for Labour Economics, 1983); William Keegan, *Mrs Thatcher's Economic Experiment* (Harmondsworth: Penguin, 1984).
2 OECD, *Economic Outlook*, Paris, June 1985.
3 C. J. Allsopp, 'The Economic Impact of North Sea Oil in the UK', paper presented to the symposium 'Lessons from Europe and Australia', Royal Commission on Federalism and Development, Ottawa, June 1984.
4 Central Statistical Office, *Economic Trends*, June 1985.
5 OECD, *Historical Statistics*, Paris, 1984.
6 NEDO, 'Trade Patterns and Industrial Change' (84) 21, 1984.
7 G. Dosi and L. Soete, 'Technology Gaps, Cost-Related Adjustments and International Trade', *Metroeconomica*, 1984.
8 H. Katrak, 'Labour-skills, R&D and Capital Requirements in the International Trade and Investment of the UK 1968–78', NIESR, August 1982.
9 NEDO, 'Trade Patterns and Industrial Change'; British Invisible Exports Council, evidence to House of Lords Select Committee on Overseas Trade, 20 March 1985.
10 Rt Hon. Nigel Lawson, Chancellor of the Exchequer, speech to the Cambridge Energy Conference, April 1984.
11 Lord Kaldor, speech to the House of Lords, 13 November 1984.
12 OECD, *Employment, Growth and Structural Change*, Paris, 1985.

13 L. Mendis and J. Muellbauer, 'British Manufacturing Productivity 1953–1983: Measurement Problems, Oil Shocks and Thatcher Effects', Discussion Paper 32, Centre for Economic Policy Research, 1985.

14 OECD, *Employment, Growth and Structural Change.*

15 IMF and OECD statistics; Morgan Guaranty, 'World Financial Markets', 1984.

5 False Dawns, False Explanations

1 Bernard D. Nossiter, *Britain: A Future that Works* (London: André Deutsch, 1978).

2 A. Hamilton, 'North Sea Impact', International Institute for Economic Research, 1978.

3 OECD, *Economic Outlook*, Paris, June 1985.

4 Speech to the House of Lords, November 1984.

5 Douglas Jay, *The Pound Sterling* (London: Sidgwick & Jackson, 1985).

6 Charter for Jobs, 'We Can Cut Unemployment', Employment Institute, March 1985.

7 Joseph A. Schumpeter, *Captialism, Socialism and Democracy*, 2nd edn (London: George Allen & Unwin, 1976).

6 Re-employing Britain

1 Douglas Jay, *The Pound Sterling* (London: Sidgwick & Jackson, 1985).

2 Cf. John Llewellyn, Stephen Potter and Lee Samuelson, *Economic Forecasting and Policy* (London: Routledge & Kegan Paul, 1985).

3 CBI Quarterly Industrial Surveys, 1985.

7 A Change of Policy

1 Ian Gilmour, *Britain Can Work* (Oxford: Martin Robertson, 1983).

2 Sir Douglas Wass, comment on Professor Geoffrey Maynard's 'Macroeconomic Aspects of the Rise and Fall in UK Oil Self-Sufficiency', Policy Studies Institute conference, London, December 1984, re-

printed in Robert Belgrave and Margaret Cornell (eds.), *Energy Self-Sufficiency for the UK*, Joint Studies in Public Policy (London: Gower, 1985).

3 Department of Energy, *Development of the Oil and Gas Resources of the United Kingdom 1985* (London: HMSO, 1985).

4 Sir Alec Cairncross, interview with author, Radio Three, August 1984.

5 George F. Will, 'If you pinch the middle class, it riots', *International Herald Tribune*, 11 December 1984.

6 Charter for Jobs, 'We Can Cut Unemployment', Employment Institute, March 1985.

Postscript

1 Frank Blackaby (ed.), *Deindustrialization* (London: NIESR, Heinemann, 1979).

2 Central Statistical Office, *Economic Trends*, June 1985; Lord Kaldor, speech to the House of Lords, November 1984.

3 OECD, *Employment, Growth and Structural Change*, Paris, 1985; L. Mendis and J. Muellbauer, 'British Manufacturing Productivity 1953–1983: Measurement Problems, Oil Shocks and Thatcher Effects', Discussion Paper 32, Centre for Economic Policy Research, 1985.

4 Knut Borchardt, 'Wirtschaftliches Wachstum und Wechsellagen 1800–1914', in H. Aubin and W. Zorn (eds.), *Handbuch der deutschen Wirtschafts- und Sozialgeschichte*, Vol. 2 (Stuttgart, 1976), cited in Carl-Ludwig Holtfrerich, 'The "Energy Crisis" in Historical Perspective', in *Studies on Economic and Monetary Problems and on Banking History*, No. 19, Deutsche Bank, 1982.

Index